THE DELIGHTFUL AUTHOR of "Where to Take Your Guests in Southern California" is a voice of experience. She, like most Southlanders, has had out of town visitors descend, wanting to see all there is in Southern California in 72 hours.

Nancy Meyer is a native of Southern California, she is a graduate of UCLA, has been published in numerous newspapers and magazines. This is her first book.

Los Angeles County Museum of Art

WHERE TO TAKE
YOUR GUESTS IN
SOUTHERN CALIFORNIA

BY NANCY MEYER

WARD RITCHIE PRESS · LOS ANGELES

For my husband, Larry Meyer
and my friend, Jane Howland
with thanks

The material in this book is reviewed and updated
at each printing.

The color photograph on the cover of this book of the
Los Angeles Music Center complex, and most of the
black and white photographs in this book, are by Jon Ritchie.

Second printing, 1974

CONTENTS

Miracle Mile

INTRODUCTION

Sooner or later it happens to everyone. After moving to Los Angeles, as much to get away from parents, inlaws and outgrown friends as to pursue "the good life" in Southern California, you're going to get the word. From Mom and Dad in Jersey; from Uncle John and Aunt Sarah in Des Moines; from brother Bill, his little woman and four kids in Nashville; from your old fraternity brother in Portland. They're coming to vacation in Southern California. With *you!*

No need to panic. Southern California hospitality being what it is, you offer to make reservations at a nearby motel, lay in a supply of beer and instant spaghetti sauce and check the hours at your local fried-chicken emporium.

But now the big question: Where do you take these eager invaders to show them the sights which, quite honestly, you haven't had time to really see yourself? How do you choose from among all the amusement attractions spreading from Magic Mountain in Valencia to Sea World at Mission Bay? From all the galleries, museums, missions and gardens stretching from Santa Barbara to San Diego? From the urban bustle of downtown Los Angeles to a quiet day at a sandy cove upcoast? Should you drive up to the Antelope Valley to tour an old gold mine or swing down to Tijuana for a plaster of Paris Venus?

Such decisions depend upon where your guests hail from, their traveling experiences, and upon their tastes and yours. And tastes do change. A generation ago most people wanted to see orange groves, Pasadena, Catalina Island and Forest Lawn. Now more and more want to visit Disneyland, the *Queen Mary,* Lion Country Safari and Sea World. Nearly all ask to see the mighty Pacific, while too many completely ignore the majestic mountains and peaceful deserts within easy reach of the city.

This brief volume is not offered as a catalogue of the multitude of pleasures available in Los Angeles and Southern California. Due to space limitations, many worthy sights and recreational activities (like participatory and spectator sports) have regrettably gone entirely without mention. Short shrift has undeservedly been given communities like Solvang, Ojai and Santa Barbara (a romantic corner of old California that's good to escape to on a hot summer day—or on any day for that matter). And such questions as where to find good dining and entertainment have been dealt with only in passing.

Rather, this book is intended as a selective and evaluative (if not always reverent) guide to help you decide where to take your special guests—to give them a view of what is typical and unusual, what is sublime and profane, how to bring a fresh eye to some well-worn sights, and how to discover others they didn't know existed.

Detailed schedules of hours and prices have not been included because they can be as changeable as the names of nightclubs on the Sunset Strip. (Even phone numbers have a way of becoming outdated as soon as printed.) So it is strongly recommended that you consult local newspapers or the Southern California Visitors Council for current information. And do call your destinations to confirm that they will be open before embarking on a day's outing.

Should your guests arrive when employment or other responsibilities prevent you from acting as a personal guide, give them this book—and a good set of maps. And if they come without wheels, direct them to Gray Line Tours or American Sightseeing.

Don't forget to watch for news of annual events like the Renaissance Pleasure Faire (which comes up each May in Agoura) or to hunt down a Bob's Big Boy hamburger joint if that's what your visitors have been counting on.

Whenever possible, try to visit major attractions on weekdays and save the less popular sights for weekends and holidays. And remember, it's far more pleasant and memorable to see three or four places thoroughly at leisure rather than race hurriedly through a dozen.

Any way you cut it, Southern California is a mighty big pie. You may already have a list of favorite places to take out of town guests. But with luck and a little experimentation, this book may help you add to that list.

The banner on the station reads: DEPOT MAIN STREET PLAZA

Disneyland

I FIRST THINGS FIRST

With most guests the problem of what to do the first day is already settled. Regardless of age, they'll probably want to start with Disneyland, even if they went just last year.

Chances are on the second day they'll want to see "Hollywood." They won't understand why you've never bumped into Ann-Margret at the supermarket or been seated near Rock Hudson at your favorite steak house. And don't bother to explain that there are nine million people in the "Greater Los Angeles" area—an area that covers at least 4000 square miles. Simply take them, or send them, to Universal City.

Come the third day, however, comes the dilemma. "After Disneyland and Hollywood," says Bernard Johnson of American Sightseeing & Tours, "it's all up for grabs." Maybe *your* guests are ready to stroll along the beach, contemplate Old Masters at the County Museum of Art or explore a musty adobe. Maybe. But it's still the age of McLuhan and the massage, and most vacationers in Southern California—the self-proclaimed "entertainment capital of the world"—are looking for ready-made amusements. And with the powers of publicity and hearsay being what they are, you'll likely choose your next destination from among the other big-name attractions included in this chapter.

DISNEYLAND

To many tourists and residents, Disneyland *is* Los Angeles (though it's actually located in Anaheim, about 25 miles south of L.A. in Orange County). While Nikita Khrushchev was once

11

Knott's Berry Farm

denied admission because adequate security protection could not be guaranteed, humbler folk wait for years for a weekend at The Magic Kingdom. Busloads of senior citizens regularly debouch at the Main Street U.S.A. portal to "the happiest place on earth." And each year youths from over 500 high schools (including several from Hawaii) watch dawn break over Sleeping Beauty Castle—a heavenly end to their "grad nite" celebrations. Gray Line even offers a four-hour tour to Disneyland which—subtracting about an hour and a half on the freeway—allows "just time to visit those one or two attractions you especially want to see."

Only the most hard-bitten cynics fail to surrender—at least temporarily—to the Disney spell. For here, whether gliding along a jungle river, rubbing elbows with life-like ghosts, twirling dizzily in the Mad-Hatter's Tea Cups or merely resting on a bench watching the Mississippi River Boat churn 'round the bend of Tom Sawyer Island, impending divorces, arthritic pains, slumping stock quotations, stubborn cases of acne and other grim realities become mere phantasms. Some even find saving grace in Disneyland. Reverend Thom Piper of Van Nuys' First Baptist Church said he was with a man who got down on his knees and accepted Christ in Tomorrowland.

On the other hand, more than a few visitors leave with a vague feeling that all is not right. Perhaps it's the absence of moral shadings. As one tourist said, "I suddenly realized that Captain Hook seemed just as attractive and heroic as Peter Pan. And the Pirates of the Caribbean—they were only *pretending* to be bad."

The transformation of reality into fantasy is also evident in Bear Country, the newest theme land. Billed as a "recreation of the Great Northwest," the four-acre area adjoining Frontierland has, maybe significantly, replaced the Indian Village. Now the

13

main feature is an entertaining 15-minute musical show called Country Bear Jamboree. The music is right out of northwest Nashville, and as for real bears, forget it. (They're at the L.A. Zoo and Japanese Village and Deer Park.) "We didn't want just plain, ordinary bears," explained one member of the Audio-Animatronics team that "imagineered" the show, "so we cartooned them up in the true Disney style." There's Teddi Barra, Trixie the Tampa Temptation and a host of other cutesy-woodsy types delivering up more wholesome family fare.

The price of escaping reality comes pretty high at Disneyland —as much as $10 per person for a day if you do it up big. Expenses can be pared by going on a summer weekend when you might wait one hour for a five-minute ride. Discount ticket books help, too. (You can spend an hour figuring out how to use them.) Or you can linger in the Main Street arcades, attend fine free shows like those presented by General Telephone, General Electric and Monsanto, or let the kids loose on Tom Sawyer Island.

You'll find Disneyland off the Santa Ana Freeway on Harbor Blvd. Just look for the Matterhorn pointing into the smog.

KNOTT'S BERRY FARM & GHOST TOWN

If your guests hanker after the Old West but can't get up to the Mother Lode country, take them to Knott's Berry Farm— the first family entertainment complex of its sort in Southern California and one that still draws nearly four million visitors a year. While exploring the ersatz 1850's-style ghost town (with its saloons, apothecaries, nickelodeons and boot hill), panning for real gold, riding a Butterfield stage or an authentic 1881 narrow-gauge train, you can turn the clock back a century and some and partake of the nostalgia and high spirits associated with the Days of Forty-nine.

14

Some people find Disneyland too perfect a product of the combined and seemingly mysterious worlds of Hollywood, engineers and artists to have a warm or homey feeling about that place. Not so at Knott's. It's a comfy spot to spend an entire day or evening—at a less frenetic pace and lower cost than at the higher-priced spread.

The reason is partly because Knott's Berry Farm is a glorious symbol of the local-boy-makes-good variety of success story that middle-Americans love so much. Walter Knott, his late wife Cordelia and their kin have run the "farm" as just folks—like you and me and Aunt Minnie. Through hard work, honesty (and some say patriotism) they parlayed a 28-acre loganberry farm begun in 1920 on mostly rented land into a successful boysenberry farm and then into the present 150-acre center for fun, inspiration and education.

The park is wonderfully eclectic, with a mish-mash of attractions appealing to all ages. There's a "live" volcano, a Spanish-Mexicanish Fiesta Village, a chapel whose "transfigured" Christ has eyes that follow you, a seven-eighths-scale, "brick-by-brick" replica of Philadelphia's Independence Hall, a gypsy camp without pickpockets. And, most recently, a theater billing top-name entertainment on weekends named after America's own John Wayne—a Walter Knott hero.

The "farm"—which no longer produces berries, by the way—is located on Beach Blvd. in Buena Park, just down the road apiece from Disneyland. Closed Christmas.

UNIVERSAL STUDIOS

In 1915, the year *Birth of a Nation* was released and almost 20 years before Cordelia Knott started serving chicken dinners at the Knott farm, Carl Laemmle turned a chicken ranch in the San Fernando Valley into Universal City. Called the "world's

Universal Studios

largest motion picture and television facility," the 420-acre city is located near Campo de Cahuenga, the site where Andres Pico signed the 1847 treaty with Mexico ceding California to the Union. Home of *Airport* and *Earthquake, Kojak* and *The Six Million Dollar Man,* Universal is the only movie studio currently offering daily behind-the-scenes tours to the general public. And it's also the most convenient and satisfying way to let your star-struck guests get *into* Hollywood.

Frankly, many Angelenos find the two-hour GlamorTram tour a little boring. "It's not that we feel superior to the Hollywood thing," one resident explains. "It's just that Los Angeles itself is one great outdoor studio." That's true, of course. We have props like the *Queen Mary* at Long Beach and the London Bridge at Lake Havasu. We have false-fronted restaurants like the Queens Arms in Encino, and false-fronted factories like Uniroyal's Babylonian palace off the Santa Ana Freeway near Atlantic Blvd. We have plastic foliage at our gas stations and "plastic" whaling villages at our harbors. Some of our neighborhoods have a Swiss chalet next to a Southern mansion next to a Mediterranean villa next to a Tudor cottage.

Still, visiting movie and TV fans (over 6 years) find the tour very exciting. Here they are shown the "secrets" of production —how a house can be made to "burn," how flash floods, thunder storms and even avalanches are created on sets from their favorite shows. They may even see a star or two (if the tour guide points them out) and be "filmed" in a cutaway car. It's all inside dope to tell the folks back home.

After the tram ride, ticket-holders may spend as much time as they like at the Entertainment Center. Here are movie props against which to have pictures taken, food booths, a stunning view of the east San Fernando Valley and at least five different shows and demonstrations. Most popular is the stunt show

17

Queen Mary

where some of the more talented but less idolized actors take high falls off roofs and punch the guts out of each other.

Found just off the Hollywood Freeway at Lankershim Blvd., Universal suggests visitors plan about a four-hour stay at the city. This leaves time to cap off the whole Hollywood fling with a drive along Hollywood Boulevard and the Sunset Strip (see Chapter 2).

QUEEN MARY

The upper decks of the *Queen Mary,* one of Southern California's newest tourist attractions, offer a delightful and instructive view. From the bow of the 81,237-ton ship you can see the surprisingly lovely Long Beach skyline. And from the stern of the world's largest passenger vessel you may notice several inviting palm-dotted islands from which seem to rise modern, pastel-colored apartment houses.

The skyline is real. So are the water, sailboats and waterskiers seven stories below. The islands and palms won't disappear. But the "apartments" are actually clever camouflage hiding huge oil rigs that pump up black gold from under the sea. Charming as they appear to out-of-towners, they are reminders of the controversy that surrounded the May, 1971 opening of the *Queen Mary* when she came permanently to rest in Long Beach Harbor after a glamorous and heroic 33-year career as a luxury liner and World War II troop transport. The idea of buying the famous Cunard ship in 1967 for $3.5 million and converting it into a museum-hotel-restaurant-gift shop center was not particularly controversial. Locals accepted it as a typical Southern California venture. But it was the cumulative costs (likely to run well over $100 million) and the financing, which involves the use of Long Beach's share of tidelands oil profits.

Such hassles may be forgotten, though, as you stroll through

Marineland

the elegant, three-story-high main lounge, or view first-class suites with 1930's *moderne* furnishings, officers' quarters, troop accommodations, the glittering bridge and the promenade and sun decks. If you don't suffer from claustrophobia, you may also wish to explore the labyrinthine engine room and see the only remaining 16-foot-diameter propeller. Then there's the interior Queen Mary Museum where old Movietone films and other memorabilia take you back 40 years. For extra money you may enter The Living Sea, an exciting array of scientific exhibits on ocean life and possible future uses of the sea, originally designed with Jacques Cousteau, and now including aquaria and tide pools.

Though still undergoing renovations, the ship has at least two restaurants and several snack bars in operation. Located along Pier J at the end of the Long Beach Freeway, the "Albatross Queen," as *Newsweek* once called her, is open every day. Sea breezes can be chilly, so take a wrap.

MARINELAND OF THE PACIFIC/SEA WORLD

If your guests have already visited an aquatic park and think when you've seen one porpoise you've seen 'em all, you may want to bypass Marineland. And if they find the sight of a penguin on roller skates, a chimpanzee on waterskis or a two-ton killer whale wearing sunglasses offensive, you might want to forget Sea World as well.

Both feature truly thrilling shows in which intelligent whales, dolphins, sea lions and sea elephants manage to maintain their dignity while performing challenging tricks men have taught them. Both are found in picturesque settings—Marineland on a rugged Palos Verdes bluff overlooking the Pacific, Sea World on San Diego's Mission Bay. Both have extensive aquaria, where you can eyeball colorful creatures from the deep, and touch-and-leave tanks for feeding and petting dolphins, walruses and

Sea World

other lovable marine relatives. Both also have sky towers that soar over 300 feet, revealing dazzling vistas on clear days.

Given a choice, however, Sea World seems to have the edge. Instead of hard expanses of concrete, Sea World is a beautiful grassy park with tree-shaded paths that wind by waterfalls and inviting ponds. Following the example of Disneyland—and with large doses of show biz—the Mission Bay site also aims at total family entertainment. For those who tire of aquatic shows and exhibits, there are craftsmen's shops, a Japanese village with pearl-diving demonstrations, a dove pavilion, hydrofoil and sky gondola rides and attractive picnic and playground areas.

Marineland, on the other hand, is less inspired by Hollywood and strives for more naturalism. The super thing here is a collossal 540,000-gallon tank called "the world's largest fishbowl." Measuring 100 feet long and 22 feet deep, the tank is stocked with 3000 fish which are hand-fed by divers several times each day. Some people stand for hours (there are 170 windows on 3 levels), apparently hypnotized as they watch leopard sharks, moray eels and giant sea bass perform graceful, unrehearsed water ballets.

LION COUNTRY SAFARI

It's been said that the only culture in Southern California is pop culture and that Southlanders are always on the hunt for a culture hero. For a while the local idol was Frasier, "the sensuous lion." Rescued from a Mexican circus that went kaput, the nearly toothless and bedraggled lion found new vitality at Lion Country Safari. At the age of about 75 on a human scale, he sired 33 cubs in 16 months—a phenomenal feat. Fan clubs sprang up all over the country, and Frasier T-shirts joined "happy face" shirts at shopping centers. Down the San Diego Freeway from the Laguna Hills wildlife preserve, men at Lei-

AIR CONDITIONED
RADIO EQUIPPED

Lion Country Safari

sure World retirement community raised their chins a little higher. Alas, Frasier has now died—happy.

Lion Country is the place to go if you want to know how it feels to live in a zoo. There's a marvelous turnabout of justice here: it's *Homo sapiens* that are locked up in mobile cages while over 125 other species happily roam free. The time to take your guests is early on a cool weekday morning when other tourists are just clearing away breakfast dishes and the animals (over 1500 of them) are fresh. Then you can feel a sense of adventure and danger when some of the more than 100 lions walk right up to your car. You might have to stop to let zebras or giraffes pass, or find yourself surrounded by a pack of cheetahs (the largest group outside of Africa). You can pull off to the side of the nominal three-lane road to identify such antelope as fringe-eared oryx, topi and brindled gnu, or watch elephants, white rhinos and hippos take their morning bath. And you can almost count on having impudent ostriches peck at your windows.

Windows, by the way, have to be rolled up with no more than about a one-inch open space. So if your car is packed with excited breathing bodies, you'll soon find the temperature rising and air in ever shorter supply. And if you make the mistake of going on a crowded afternoon when the route is jammed with cars, campers and sightseeing buses, claustrophobia can set in quickly. Then you'll look forward to reaching the entertainment area where you can stretch your legs, buy food and drinks and let restless kids go on rides.

The admission seems more than a mite expensive for the typical hour-and-a-half tour. And detailed souvenir booklets and tape-recorded guides both come at extra charge. But if you're looking for Africa, it's just off the San Diego Freeway at Moulton Parkway where the sign reads: "NO TRESPASSING, VIOLATORS WILL BE EATEN!"

25

Los Angeles Zoo

LOS ANGELES ZOO AND GRIFFITH PARK

There's a rumor in town that prospective Sierra Club hikers go to the Los Angeles Zoo to get in shape. If it isn't true, it could be. For the zoo (third largest in the nation with over 3000 animals of more than 1000 species) spreads out over 80 acres, and most of them seem to be uphill. To be sure, there are some down-hill paths and a number of tree-shaded benches to rest on. But there's always another crest to climb—even to get out of the zoo. For extra charge you can board a nonguided minibus that swings around the perimeter of the five major continental areas, depositing passengers at stop points (from which they must begin the hike again).

Though the L.A. Zoo definitely comes off second best when compared to the great San Diego facility, it does have its charms. There's an open, airy feel in the park, and canyon breezes waft away all but a few of the organic smells. Since opening in 1966 at its new location in the northeast corner of Griffith Park, the trees, shrubs and flower beds have at last begun to grow into proportion with the concrete housing structures—most of them open, moated enclosures.

Guests with kids in tow will want to stop at the children's zoo. Located near the entrance, this area features a seal tank, a tunnel of nocturnal creatures, and a "happy hollow" where city-bred youngsters can feed and pet barnyard animals—and maybe lose their zoo maps to fearless goats with undiscriminating appetites. Here, too, is a nursery where you might see infant chimps, bears or other newborn mammals in incubators or playpens only inches away.

The zoo is only one of many attractions within 4063-acre Griffith Park—the eastern terminus of the Santa Monica Mountains. If you have time and energy left after visiting the zoo, stop at Travel Town on the north side on Forest Lawn Dr. There's

27

Busch Gardens

no charge here to climb in and over old trains, trolleys and airplanes or to explore the museum with its venerable fire engines, milk trucks and models of ships and planes.

Or on a hot, smoggy day, motor around to Fern Dell on the park's south side. Your guests will probably feel refreshed as they walk through this lengthy retreat where streams splash about the lush foliage. Or drive up to the top of the park to the Observatory and Planetarium. Planetarium shows are often rather good, and the free museum has an array of educational exhibits (many with buttons to push) and a pendulum that swings hypnotically. Should you come on that proverbial clear day, your guests will have one of the best looks at the city from this peak, though the view is usually better at night.

BUSCH GARDENS

A few years ago, L.A. residents were provoked to a mighty public outrage when $74,000 worth of plastic plants were installed along a one-mile median strip on Jefferson Boulevard. But few visitors cry "plastic" at Busch Gardens, though this exotic St. Louis beer dream is as unnatural an Eden as man has devised. The lovely lakes and waterways are antiseptically clean and insect-free. Most of the lush flora and colorful fauna are tropical or subtropical imports. Mono Lake "featherock" boulders used in the piney gorge area are so light they must be moored to the bottom of the lagoon. And the macaws are rounded up each night lest they deleaf all the trees or be done in by marauding house cats.

Hokey as it may be, Busch Gardens can be a delightful place to take your guests—especially if they're older folk from Indiana, garden freaks, or if they've never seen what wonders water can work in arid land. Thanks to a five-acre expansion opened in 1972, there's more to do now at the verdant ad-

Magic Mountain

junct to Anheuser-Busch's brewery (on Roscoe Boulevard just off the San Diego Freeway in the San Fernando Valley): Brewery tours (hardly worth the time), monorail and flume rides (something for the kids), trained bird shows and animal acts, a walk-through aviary, otter and penguin exhibits, snack bars—plus generous samples of suds.

All this was free until the company decided to "commercially diversify into the field of leisure-time activity and family entertainment." Now the cost runs about the equivalent of two six-packs per adult, which is small charge for a trip to the South Seas without ever leaving Southern California.

MAGIC MOUNTAIN

When Magic Mountain opened its gates in May, 1971, someone forgot to push the magic button. The heavily publicized antique carousel never did work during the first season at Southern California's newest family entertainment center, and other new rides occasionally broke down due to unexpected mechanical snafus. So many people made the 35-mile drive north to Valencia from downtown Los Angeles that the young, inexperienced staff couldn't handle the crowds of thrill-seekers. Management had its problems, too. Public relations and ad men were hired and fired so fast many thought they were on a three-minute merry-go-round ride.

Since then, millions of dollars have been wisely spent expanding and improving the grounds, adding new attractions and comforts. Certainly the park's chief magic trick—water—is working well. It bubbles and sprays, cascades and splashes about the 200-acre hill, turning the brown earth into a parkland with over two million square feet of lawns, trees and flowering plants.

Aquatics and greenery aside, Magic Mountain is essentially a

31

Forest Lawn

clean, updated version of an old-fashioned amusement park, with thrill rides, gondola rides, a monorail, a sky tower, a tots' section, a row of carny games, an air-conditioned, sit-down restaurant, numerous snack bars, dancing pavilions and theaters where show folk and variety acts provide outdoor entertainment for all ages. Best of all, the one-price admission fee ($5.50 for adults; $4.50 for 3-to-12 years) allows unlimited use of all facilities (except, of course, games, foods, souvenirs and the like).

Magic Mountain is no place to be caught on a summer afternoon when temperatures often surpass 100 degrees. Far better to plan your visit here for a summer evening or a cool, off-season weekend afternoon. A great place for teenagers.

FOREST LAWN MEMORIAL PARK

"The man at the information booth said if I took every left turn and drove fast I could just make the 1 o'clock crucifixion and resurrection. I did. And it was nice—*real* nice." So a gentleman was heard to say upon leaving Los Angeles' necrophilic wonderland. Yes, even crucifixions are "nice" at Glendale's home branch of Forest Lawn—the mortuary and memorial park founded by Hubert Eaton who said in his Builder's Creed: "I believe, most of all, in a Christ that smiles and loves you and me."

The Crucifixion, of course, is Jan Styka's 195-by-45-foot painting of the moment *before* Christ was nailed to the cross. *The Resurrection* is another sizable painting—this one by Robert Clark who was commissioned to do the work when Dr. Eaton searched the world's art and found no representation of the event "realistic" enough or "suitable for an American audience."

Forest Lawn, which "serves 20 families each day," is best known for its collection of artistic and architectural reproductions. There's da Vinci's *Last Supper* in stained glass, many of Michelangelo's statuary (including *Moses* and *David*) and churches, such as the Wee Kirk O' the Heather (a replica of Annie Laurie's church and a favorite for weddings).

The envy of every suburban gardener who tries to keep his lawn green in winter, the cemetery welcomes visitors—more than one million a year. But it does have rules to protect "property owners." Like no shorts (smocks are available), no dogs or radios outside cars, no solicitation "of any kind for any purpose," no picnicking or lying on the grass, no roller skates or scooters. "After all," a Glendale resident explained, "it's supposed to be like going to church—and they don't want it to be a Disneyland for the dead, you know."

2 STAR STRUCK

Making a pilgrimage to Hollywood is so passé it's almost "in" again. So if your guests were thrilled with the slick Universal Studios tour but say now they'd like to see the *real* Hollywood, don't be embarrassed for them. While tinsel town is slightly tarnished these days, a tour of Hollywood proper and a drive along Sunset Boulevard can still be exciting—not to mention startling or enlightening.

HOLLYWOOD CEMETERY

The pilgrimage begins at the Hollywood Cemetery, 6000 Santa Monica Blvd., about ten blocks west of the Hollywood Freeway. Somewhat off the current tourist path, the cemetery certainly is no Forest Lawn. There are headstones here, many tilted askew, and on weekends young lads sometimes explore the quiet grounds, peering into newly dug graves while their dogs urinate on withered potted plants. Behind the administration building (where you can get maps of the cemetery) you might see an ancient car or two, grounded on flat tires. And you may even glimpse a solitary woman, attired in her Sunday best, carrying red roses to place on the grave of some former idol. For, scattered throughout the grounds are monuments to such greats as Douglas Fairbanks, Sr., Rudolph Valentino, Marion Davies, Tyrone Power, Cecil B. DeMille, as well as others whose names were once the talk of the town. *Sic transit gloria*. Sorry, but the old Hollywood is dead.

Hollywood Cemetery

HOLLYWOOD BOULEVARD

Meanwhile, up on Hollywood Boulevard, the new Hollywood is very much alive. On weekdays local residents come here to shop—from expensive homes in the nearby hills, from ritzy and tacky apartment houses, from old stucco or frame bungalows found just off the thoroughfare. On weekend nights outsiders flock to theaters like the Pantages and the Egyptian, to the Hollywood Palladium and, in summer, to the nearby Hollywood Bowl. And any time of day or night you encounter street people —of all colors, modes of dress and sexual persuasions. Some are looking for a handout. Others, addressing you with "Peace, brother," hand out religious tracts. The street's alive. Bizarrely so.

HOLLYWOOD AND VINE

Despite all warnings, eastern tourists are almost invariably disappointed with downtown Hollywood. The string of second-rate clothing stores and has-been apartments that line the usual approach (along Hollywood Boulevard from the freeway) soon dispel any notion that this is the glamor capital of the world. And the magic corner of Hollywood and Vine does indeed look like the center of Anytown, U.S.A.

But it isn't. One-half block north on Vine rises the circular, 13-story Capitol Records Building, looking like a stack of giant discs. Across from it is the ABC Hollywood Palace, a theater where live TV shows draw the faithful. And to the south is one of the famous Brown Derby restaurants and the Huntington Hartford Theatre which books traveling dramatic and musical shows.

GRAUMAN'S CHINESE THEATRE

Several blocks westward, katty-corner from the Hollywood

Roosevelt Hotel, is the city's chief shrine—Grauman's Chinese Theatre. Once the host to gala film premieres, the garish theater's arcade is always crowded with friendly, impressionable tourists. "Would ya look at these weird thumbs!" they'll say, pointing to Jimmy Stewart's handprints. "How sweet. Shirley Temple's feet. And she was only eight years old." "Oh, look! Here's Roy Rogers' gun, and Joe E. Brown's mouth! Isn't it *wonderful!*" It *is* a wonderful place to eavesdrop, and for a quarter you can get a wax Buddha souvenir—if the machine is working.

HOLLYWOOD WAX MUSEUM

Just one block east there is more wax—a whole gallery of it! The figures in the darkened, somewhat shabby interior tend to be powdery and less lifelike than those at the larger Movieland Wax Museum and Palace of Living Art in Buena Park. But you can see a strange potpourri of personalities here: old stars and new idols, American presidents and western frontiersmen, and quasi-historical scenes like the Yalta Conference (with Hitler and Mussolini present!). You can scream in a chamber of horrors or feel a catch in your throat as you press a phone to your ear and hear again the voice of John Kennedy. You can even sit a spell and watch flickering films that tell the story of the Academy Awards from 1927 to the present. And if religion's your thing, there's the *Last Supper,* the *Pietà,* Junípero Serra, Mahatma Gandhi and Moses (as played by Charlton Heston, that is).

WALK OF FAME

You're not likely to see any movie stars at Grauman's. But thanks to the Hollywood Chamber of Commerce, you can at least take the Walk of Fame. Enshrined in brass stars set in terrazzo along Hollywood Boulevard and part of Vine are the names of over 1500 stars of TV, film and radio. When Charlie Chaplin returned to the States in 1972 after a 20-year exile, he was finally honored with a star at the corner of Hollywood Boulevard and McCadden. Apparently his leftish leanings and private peccadillos seem less offensive in the 70s than they did in 1956 when the walk was begun. At least 80 other names still await installation—a chore that costs about $1000 per. "I suppose it isn't kosher to say this," a Chamber man said, "but we'd sure appreciate contributions." Julie Andrews fans, take note!

LOOKING DOWN ON HOLLYWOOD

For a loftier perspective of the Hollywood scene you can go to Oscar's, a revolving restaurant atop the 23-story Holiday Inn one-half block north from Grauman's. From here you get a glittery view of Los Angeles by night and an incomparable peek into the Hollywood Hills. Waitresses can point out the Magic Castle, an old mansion that is now a private club for magicians and wizardry buffs. And on the hill above it you can see Yamashiro—an imposing pagoda-like palace that was the haunt of the exclusive Club of the 400 in the twenties and location for parts of the movie *Sayonara*. Now a restaurant-bar complex housing Oriental art treasures, Yamashiro is a good place to go for a drink—the price of an unusual view and a story to tell the folks back home. (Take Sycamore Avenue from Franklin Avenue.)

SUNSET STRIP

Like Hollywood proper, the Strip has known better times. In the good old days, say 30 years ago, the stars came here to visit their agents, to party at the Garden of Allah, to see and be seen. The Garden of Allah has been razed and replaced with a bank, and the stars have scattered all over the world. Even the hippies

Grauman's Chinese Theatre

and Jesus freaks have moved on, though you may spot a late-blooming flower child or two.

Still, a pilgrimage to Starland should include a drive—preferably in a convertible—along this two-mile stretch of county territory roughly bounded by the old Schwabs drugstore at the corner of Laurel Canyon and the new Schwabs near the corner of Doheny. Here you can see a lot—Las Vegas-style billboards advertising the latest film release or rock group, swank old buildings like the Sunset Tower apartments, expensive boutiques in the Sunset Plaza area, and a collection of here-today-gone-tomorrow head shops, massage parlors, discotheques and rock groupie hangouts. There are also a number of sidewalk cafes where hairy-chested men with shirts open to the waist sit with scantily clad lasses whose legs dangle within view of the stop-and-go traffic, and several fine restaurants, including Scandia, The Imperial Gardens, The Aware Inn, Cock n' Bull and the Kavkaz, where people actually *do* see stars, or reasonable facsimiles.

By day the street has a distinctly seedy look, and at night the Strip is heavy on strip. At the Classic Cat, The Body Shop, The Phone Booth and other possibly less permanent establishments, the girls are not simply nude. As one marquee put it, they are "stark naked." Topless, bottomless girlie revues may not be what Aunt Emma wants to see in Los Angeles. But Uncle John may want to check it out . . . perhaps on amateur night.

BEVERLY HILLS HOMES

Traveling westward on Sunset Boulevard, there's no question where the Strip ends. As soon as you see the Beverly Hills sign implanted in the parkway, you know you've entered another world. Not because of the sign—which is old and quaint and easy to miss. But because of the lavish homes that begin here

41

Beverly Hills

and continue almost uninterrupted for miles and miles through Beverly Hills, Holmby Hills, Bel-Air, Westwood, Brentwood and Pacific Palisades—all the way to the sea at Malibu.

Here and there you may notice newer signs, too, like "Beware, Sentry Dogs on Duty." All reminders that here are the most admired and despised symbols of the American Dream—huge mansions of every architectural style and historical period where, you tell the children, "the rich people live." Some homes, like those along Sunset Boulevard itself, are prominently set on knolls overlooking acres of immaculate lawns or vast expanses of Algerian ivy. Others, particularly north of the boulevard, are tucked away in the hills behind walls of trees and flowering shrubs. (For an easterner, the flora will be as impressive as the homes he cannot see.)

Even if your guests are not celebrity crazed, a drive through Beverly Hills may well be one of the most vivid memories of their visit to Southern California. If you have only a half-hour or so, cruise along Sunset Boulevard past the elegant Beverly Hills Hotel as far as UCLA. Then return the same way, passing Jayne Mansfield's last home (at 10100 Sunset Blvd.) and take a few turns down streets like Bedford, Camden, Rodeo or Beverly Drive. Or turn north of Sunset into the ritzier district, say on Whittier past Paul Newman and Joanne Woodward's former home (at 907). Make a right on Lexington one block and you'll be at Lucille Ball's house, 1000 N. Roxbury. Chances are you'll find a line of cars here. Necks crane, station wagons unload, cameras click. (Should you come by on Halloween you'd probably see an incredibly long queue of kids—trucked in from the suburbs to collect what their parents consider very special treats.)

If these addresses are important to your guests, suggest they take a bus tour. Instead of struggling with maps, nearly running

Farmers Market

down a housemaid walking the family poodles or colliding with another Plymouth full of outlanders, you get a fairly accurate and quite entertaining tour. The guides do know the territory, and if their stories are sometimes apocryphal, no matter. This is the land of make-believe.

Do-it-yourselfers can purchase maps to the stars' homes. The one-page variety available at roadside stands along Sunset Blvd. is outrageously priced at about $4 and generally difficult to follow. For about $2 you can buy booklets at most area hotels, drugstores and gas stations. Less accurate, these at least have photographs and make good souvenirs.

WHERE TO SEE THE STARS

True devotees aren't content with houses. As Bernard Johnson of American Sightseeing says, "they want to see the stars in their native habitat—and they'd much rather see one eating a hamburger than performing on the stage." One member of the Hollywood Chamber of Commerce claims he's never been at the corner of Hollywood and Vine without seeing at least one film, TV or recording personality. "The older stars' agents are right there in the Taft Building," he says. "And I've stood on the corner talking to John Wayne and nobody, *nobody* recognized him."

The problem is that off the magnified screen and off the spotlighted stage the stars are reduced to human scale. Without makeup and wigs, they look very much like the tourists who are looking for them.

But if you want to go on a star hunt, you can go to the posh Polo Lounge in the Beverly Hills Hotel—if you can carry it off. Or to the better (and expensive) restaurants like Chasens, La Scala, Musso & Frank's Grill or Martoni's. Back to those hamburgers, a UCLA student reports seeing Caesar Romero several

NBC TV studios

times at Westwood's Hamburger Hamlet, "just sitting at the counter, all alone." Others recommend opening performances at nightclubs in the area (they come to cheer their friends). And if you follow Joyce Haber, the L.A. *Times* Hollywood correspondent, you can find some clues. Like the report that Marlene Dietrich picks up fresh vegetables every day at Beverly Hills' Premier Market.

TV STUDIO TOURS & SHOW TICKETS

Your guests won't have time to stand outside a market all day on the chance they'll see Marlene Dietrich driving up in a taxi to buy a head of cabbage. If you have enough advance warning of their arrival, plan instead to take them to the filming of a TV show (and get the screening date so they can watch it later).

If you don't care what show you see, simply write CBS, NBC or ABC requesting free tickets for a specific week. (Most studios send only two tickets, so have your neighbors write at the same time for you. And expect several weeks' wait before the tickets arrive.) If you have a specific show in mind, call first to see whether or not tickets are available. You may find, as one hopeful did, that ABC's *Let's Make a Deal* has a waiting list of two and a half years! (There are lots of ordinary Americans willing to don a crazy costume and fill their pockets with hard-boiled eggs just to have a chance of winning a new freezer or a trip to "the islands.")

As an alternative, consider taking a TV studio tour. CBS at Television City, Fairfax and Beverly Boulevard, offers a free quickie—one-half hour usually each weekday afternoon. And NBC on Alameda in Burbank gives a one-hour tour every day except Sunday, for a price.

Downtown Los Angeles

3 CITY SIGHTS

After several days of long-distance commuting to popular attractions in Anaheim and Valencia, Hollywood and Long Beach, visitors sometimes ask, "But where is *Los Angeles,* and why haven't you shown us *downtown*?" It isn't an easy question to answer.

A wag once said that all American cities are Cleveland, in one guise or another. New York is Cleveland on an island, San Francisco is Cleveland on hills, and Los Angeles is Cleveland flattened by a rolling pin. Whatever that cynic's reputation for accuracy generally, Los Angeles is one enormous spread-out burg. The city does have prescribed limits—a crazy zig-zag that surrounds incorporated cities like Beverly Hills and unincorporated spots of county territory like the Sunset Strip—though not one Angeleno in a thousand could tell you where the city limits run. Indeed, everyone has his own view of where Los Angeles begins and ends. Those with a narrow north-western orientation see it as a rectangular plot of real estate following Wilshire and Sunset boulevards from downtown to Santa Monica. At the other extreme are those who consider L.A. as the entire megalopolis sprawling eastward across the basin to San Bernardino, crawling northward over the Santa Monica Mountains into the San Fernando Valley and spreading southward to encompass most of Orange County. Still others avoid the whole geographical problem by saying Los Angeles isn't so much a place as it is a way of life—however appalling that prospect may be to some.

And as for going downtown, a typical host might say "it isn't worth it." For years Angelenos avoided the moribund city core

49

with its deteriorating buildings, impossible traffic snarls, multiple skid rows, assorted freaks and self-appointed spreaders of the gospel. They seldom took guests into the area and went there themselves only when pressed to do so. Occasionally they would point out the pyramidal City Hall as they whizzed by on the Santa Ana-Hollywood Freeway, but their sights were almost always fixed on some more pleasing destination.

That was yesterday. Today, little by little, a new central city is being born. Bauhaus skyscrapers now dominate the old, low-profile cityscape. Redevelopment projects, like the 136-acre Bunker Hill area in which soars the first of a family of high-rise apartments, have already leveled many blocks of blight. A new Civic Center, with the nation's second-largest complex of city, county, state and federal buildings, faces an attractive, three-block-long mall where flags wave, fountains splash and benches await sitters. At the top of the mall is the city's pride—the $34.5 million Music Center for the Performing Arts. And these are only openers. Additional plans to further revitalize and, many hope, humanize the inner city are presently on the drawing boards.

For all its spots of ugliness, its maddening traffic and its eye-smarting smog, downtown Los Angeles is a dynamic place where more and more suburbanites actually say it is "fun" to go. One of the newer fun places is O'Shaughnessy's Restaurant, a happy Irish pub and dining spot found in the shopping arcade underneath the 52-story twin towers of the Atlantic Richfield Plaza on South Flower Street. Here, as elsewhere in central and western Los Angeles, are a number of places you can take your guests to give them a sense of urban life, to let them see the heart of the nation's third-largest city.

DOWNTOWN

Downtown Los Angeles is still a 9-to-5, Monday-to-Friday place. So for a brief, peaceful glimpse, go on Saturday or Sunday. But to show your visitors the city at work, choose a weekday—particularly during the noon hour when the "movers and shakers" come down from their offices and take to the streets enroute to three-martini lunches.

In either case, the best way to tour downtown is on foot, and a convenient starting place is at the Music Center on top of the hill between First and Temple, Hope and Grand (you can park in the Center's lots). On a relatively clear day, or at sunset, the view from this eminence is grand. And visitors from smaller cities are usually impressed by the temples here. There's the Dorothy Chandler Pavilion (a big concert hall where you can come dressed to the teeth to hear the L.A. Philharmonic in winter and spring, Civic Light Opera in summer, and an all-year series of visiting programs); the Ahmanson Theatre (a slightly smaller, rather dreary all-purpose auditorium whose balconies are not recommended for acrophobes); and the Mark Taper Forum (an intimate semi-circular theater frequently presenting new or off-beat drama—and a place you can wear anything that's "in"). Across Hope Street culture yields to the functional—and the Water and Power Building, surrounded by reflecting pools and fountains.

After strolling through the Civic Center Mall, walk down Broadway to the Grand Central Public Market, 317 S. Broadway (closed Sunday). Here you find a glorious mixture of inner-city people—blacks, chicanos, Orientals and Caucasians—shopping at over 100 open stalls for everything from fresh produce to artificial eyelashes.

Return to Third and cross Broadway to the Bradbury Build-

51

ing, 304 S. Broadway (usually closed Saturday and Sunday). From the outside this 1893 sandstone and brick structure looks unimposing—even drab. But step inside and you will discover a treasure-trove of elegance. Facing an open central court are five stories of exquisite wrought-iron balcony railings, pink marble stairways with more ornate railings, two bird-cage elevators you can ride, rich wood panelling, decorative Mexican floor tiles—and all of it crowned by a huge leaded-glass ceiling.

Walking one block east to Spring then down to the corner of Fifth puts you at the historic Alexandria Hotel. This old (1906) hostelry was once the stopping place for international celebrities and movieland stars before it fell on inglorious flophouse days. Recently restored to its original Victorian magnificence, the hotel is now something of a shrine (the stained-glass-domed Palm Court is an historic-cultural landmark) and a very chic place to go for dinner or a drink. Visitors are welcome to peek into the Valentino Room and take a nostalgic stroll through the opulent lobby with its walnut panelling, red velvet upholstery, burnished brass railings, antique furnishings and photographic displays.

Within walking distance from the Alexandria are Pershing Square, the Central Library, the *Times* Building, St. Vibiana's Cathedral and City Hall. And not far are Little Tokyo and Chinatown (see Chapter 5), Olvera Street and the Old Plaza area (see Chapter 4). But by now you may be ready to return to your car and head westward to other sights.

WILSHIRE BOULEVARD AND WEST LOS ANGELES

A tour of downtown can be missed, but you shouldn't pass up a chance to drive your guests along fabled Wilshire Boulevard— L.A.'s only answer to New York's Fifth Avenue, Paris' *Champs Elysées* and Mexico City's *Paseo de la Reforma*. Equally im-

Wilshire Boulevard

pressive by day or night, the boulevard stretches 16 miles from the congested city core (over virtually the same route followed, in turn, by mastodons, Indians, mission fathers and cattle drivers) all the way to a grassy bluff overlooking the Pacific at Santa Monica.

Not far from its downtown beginnings the boulevard cuts across MacArthur Park (where you can rent paddleboats and hear concerts in summer) and Lafayette Park (reflected again and again in the all-glass CNA Building). Then you enter the "corridor"—a high-rise, Tishmanesque chain of banks, ad agencies, western outposts of national corporations, legal firms and others who can afford to buy instant prestige with an expensive Wilshire address. On the left, at 3400, you pass the Ambassador Hotel (where the stars used to play and Robert Kennedy was shot). And on the right, at 4101, is Perino's (*the* restaurant in Los Angeles, one that L.A. *Times* restaurant editor, Lois Dwan, says "costs no more than a trip to Las Vegas" but is "infinitely better for your soul").

From La Brea to Fairfax is the section known as the Miracle Mile. It was here—in the 1920's and 1930's—that a speculator named A. W. Ross lured the first department stores and businesses away from downtown and out to the "sticks." Thus began a commercial and financial westward movement that still keeps the structural steel makers in business.

Before leaving the Mile, stop just east of Fairfax at Hancock Park to show your guests two adjacent "miracles." One is the La Brea Tar Pits, where fossilized bones of prehistoric beasts lay open to viewers (see Chapter 4). The other is the Los Angeles County Museum of Art. Until 1965, when this handsome, three-gallery monument to Culture opened, L.A.'s meager art treasures were housed in an Exposition Park museum along with La Brea fossils and mummy tombs. Since moving to Wilshire Boul-

Los Angeles County Museum of Art

evard, the permanent collection has been richly augmented with Old Masters (thanks mainly to Norton Simon) and other notable historic and contemporary works. While it isn't the Met, the gallery does offer the best around—aesthetic smorgasbord à la Los Angeles. (Art fanciers can also be directed to the Pasadena Art Museum for some modern things, the Huntington for 18th-century British and French works, the J. Paul Getty Museum for Italian and Dutch paintings and 18th-century furniture, and La Cienega's gallery row for a little something to take back home.)

As a possible measure of how far Culture has come in Los Angeles (and how far it has to go), consider these figures: On the average, the County Museum of Art welcomes about 5000 visitors each day, while just ten blocks north—on a typical day—somewhere between 20,000 and 50,000 people flock to Farmers Market. Therefore chances are quite good that your guests—or at least the ladies—will appreciate a brief side trip to the Fairfax and Third Street mart.

From the present fancy setup and sometimes astronomical prices you wouldn't guess that the market began in 1934 as an out-of-the-back-of-the-truck affair. In those hard-luck Depression days, real farmers from the San Fernando Valley (which still has a few acres of fields) came here to save themselves by selling eggs and produce to hungry city-slickers.

To satisfy all your party, time your visit here for lunch. Menfolk can enjoy a leisurely outdoor repast—some two dozen restaurants offer international fare ranging from tacos to blintzes to roast beef—while the "girls" dash off to over 150 shops with exotic and native foods and wares. (Send the kids, who are bored with all this, to the pet stores.) There's even a post office in the market where your guests can stop off to mail gifts to those they left behind.

56

Back on the westward Wilshire Boulevard drive the shopping scene becomes more exclusive. From San Vicente to Santa Monica boulevards, Wilshire slices through Beverly Hills, and along the boulevard you see banks, cinemas, delis, travel agencies—and expensive stores like Saks Fifth Avenue and I. Magnin's where those-who-got get what-they-want and never mind the price.

The rather ugly Wilshire-Santa Monica Boulevard intersection marks the western end of the Beverly Hills shopping district and the southwestern corner of the famous residential section (see Chapter 2). At this junction you might turn left several blocks to show your guests Century City. Located on 180 acres of the old Twentieth Century-Fox lot, the new office-hotel-apartment-restaurant-shopping complex is the world's largest privately financed urban development. Sounds great, yet the "city" does have its detractors, like L.A. *Times* architecture critic John Pastier who called it "a hollow parody of an urban setting, slick and imposing but ultimately inhuman." Since darkness helps cloak the sterility, the best time to bring your guests here is at night—for dinner at Señor Pico (authentic Mexican dishes) or Yamato (equally authentic Japanese cuisine), or for a theatrical evening at the new Shubert Theatre or cocktails and entertainment at the Century Plaza Hotel's Hong Kong Bar. (Elsewhere there's The Lighthouse in Hermosa Beach, Donte's in North Hollywood and Concerts by the Sea in Redondo Beach —all featuring jazz. For pop and folk there's the Troubadour, for opera concerts, La Strada—both in Los Angeles.)

The Santa Monica Boulevard intersection is also the gateway to Westwood's condominium row—another high-rise corridor where more and more well-to-do find "apartment living" elegant and easy. The upward growth stretches all the way to Westwood Village, obliterating a view of the UCLA campus which begins a

Exposition Park

few blocks northward. Old-timers who remember the charming village that grew up here in the middle of bean fields regret Westwood's new look. Yet, happy crowds filling the streets, shops, restaurants and arcades testify that, unlike Century City, it still is a place for people. It's also one of the few places in town made for walking, and is thought by some to be the most cosmopolitan spot in Los Angeles.

Continuing westward on Wilshire Boulevard, only minutes away, is the lovely palm- and pine-shaded Santa Monica Palisades, and just beyond and below lies the Pacific. Apparently only a barrier as mighty as the sea can stop the westering tilt of the Fabulous Boulevard.

EXPOSITION PARK

For hosts and guests on a budget, another possible cityside destination is Exposition Park, located a couple of miles south of downtown just off the Harbor Freeway and across Exposition Boulevard from USC. Besides the Sports Arena and the Coliseum (used during the 1932 Olympics and for Trojan, Bruin and Rams home football games), the park also contains two rather good museums. And both are free.

The Los Angeles County Museum of Natural History occupies an old three-story building that looks and smells like a museum. Here are gigantic dinosaur skeletons, hundreds of La Brea fossils (see Chapter 4), four darkened halls of animal habitat groups (the creatures neither move nor stink), dioramas and displays on California history and western Indians, a mineral exhibit in a stained-glass-domed rotunda—and much more to intrigue visitors of all ages and interests.

Not far eastward is the California Museum of Science and Industry which sprawls into several buildings, old and new, and is backed by a seven-acre rose garden with thousands of bushes of over 160 varieties. More heavily visited than the Natural History Museum, the exhibits here range from mathematics and energy to anatomy and dentistry. Many are industry-sponsored—sophisticated enough for adults but equally exciting for children. For the special thing about this museum is its methods of presentation. Called a "museum to touch," everywhere there are buttons to push, levers to pull, games to play, phones to pick up—and sometimes they all work.

WATTS TOWERS

Farther south, in the heart of the black ghetto known as south-central Los Angeles, is the community of Watts. Far removed in every imaginable way from the opulence and relative safety of Wilshire Boulevard, Watts is famous both as the site of bloody riots in 1965 and as the home of the Towers of Simon Rodia—undoubtedly the most remarkable and bizarre example of folk art in our nation.

For 33 years the Italian immigrant tile-setter worked all alone —sometimes singing arias, sometimes yelling at passersby— constructing a Marco Polo Ship, a Hall of Mirrors and three conical towers, one of which sweeps skyward almost 100 feet. Built of concentric steel rings spoked to central cores, the lacy confections are covered with cement into which Sam (as he was called) implanted sea shells, bits of tile, broken plates, glasses and bottles—in fact, almost anything other people would call junk. Some said Rodia was crazy. Sam said "I wanted to do something for the United States because there are nice people in this country."

Having finished this strange life work in 1954, Sam walked away and never returned. Four years later a group of "concerned citizens" arranged for a test to see if the towers shouldn't be demolished as safety hazards. When 10,000 pounds of pressure were applied to the main tower, the tower held but the rig broke! Since declared an historic-cultural landmark, the towers (located at 1765 E. 107th St.) are usually open from noon to dusk.

SCENIC VIEWS OF THE CITY

Anyone who has flown into International Airport on a clear night knows that Los Angeles can be an incredibly beautiful city. When the sun goes down the lid comes off the smog pot revealing a wonderland of twinkling lights stretching farther than the eye can see. Before nightfall, however, the city is often invisible—not to mention unlivable. Based on 1962-1970 averages, the Los Angeles Air Pollution Control District reports there are only about 36 days a year when visibility is over 10 miles in the Los Angeles basin.

Should your guests be with you on one of those days, or if you do your sightseeing at night, head for the Santa Monica Mountains. The best natural vantage points lie in this east-west range that separates the basin from the San Fernando Valley. If you don't mind a winding mountain road, follow Mulholland Drive as it twists along the top of the massif from the Hollywood Hills to Encino. There are a number of magnificent views of the Valley, though too few of Los Angeles proper. (Sunset Boulevard, which rides low on the Los Angeles side of the mountains, is now much too clogged with multi-story buildings and residences to offer many panoramic vistas, though restaurants like Scandia, Aware Inn and The Kavkaz have good views.) The single best lookout is from the Observatory in Griffith Park. Situated on a pinnacle at the eastern end of the Santa Monicas, this point overlooks Hollywood and all of the western Los Angeles basin. There are places to park, benches to sit on, and a free uninterrupted view.

61

For those who prefer towers to mountains, City Hall's 27th floor observation deck is open free every day. Or for rooftop dining with splendid view you can take your guests to the Tower (atop the Occidental Building on S. Hill downtown)—if you can afford it. Or to Room at the Top, in this case the top of the Sunset Vine Tower at the corner of Sunset and Vine in Hollywood.

4 POKING INTO THE PAST

To the horror of its detractors, Los Angeles has been called the ultimate city, the prototype metropolis of the future, the pace-setter for the nation—perhaps for the world. Sitting at the edge of the western frontier, it is also a very new city. Although its "civilized" Anglo history goes back all of 200-odd years, Los Angeles is really a creation of the 20th century, and true to this century, its only constant is change.

Whatever is "old" is, *ipso facto,* useless. Buildings are regularly razed, regardless of historical value or interest, to be replaced by concrete freeways, high-rise office buildings and self-contained, temperature-controlled shopping centers. The hills are carved by cut-and-fill to make way for tract houses, each one looking like the next. Orchards, orange groves and bean fields are scraped clean for stucco apartment houses expected to last maybe 40 years.

It is said that Southern Californians live for today, plan for tomorrow and never look backward. An exaggeration no doubt. Yet, historical societies notwithstanding, not many Angelenos give more than one hoot for the past. A recent Washington Birthday observance in the Civic Center drew a "crowd" of about three dozen. Back in 1965 an ancient oak, the famous hangman's tree of Calabasas, was removed so a 40-foot-wide moon rocket could pass. And only at the 11th hour in 1970 did a group of citizens manage to rescue a handful of Bunker Hill's Victorian homes before the rest were knocked down for new

63

Hancock Park, La Brea Tar Pits

glass-and-steel skyscrapers. Moved to Heritage Square just off the Pasadena Freeway near Ave. 43, the first two were burned by vandals. The others sit on blocks behind locked gates, silently watching the latest Detroit models speed by.

LA BREA TAR PITS

But Now Town has had its yesteryears. Stop at Rancho La Brea next to the County Museum of Art on Wilshire Boulevard and you can walk around a prehistoric lake where bears, lions, ground sloths, camels, wolves, birds, bison, mastodons (but no dinosaurs) contended for life at least 10,000 years ago.

Even then Los Angeles had its deceits. Beneath the pools of water was an asphalt morass that sucked unwary creatures to their Ice Age grave, thus giving the modern world its richest source of fossils. The first digs, 1906-1915, produced over one million late-Pleistocene fossils, including more than 2000 saber-toothed tiger skulls. Excavations begun in 1969 utilizing tooth-brushes and dental picks have unearthed 31,750 fossil speci-mens plus tens of thousands of microfossils. A "La Brea Woman" has been carbon-14-dated at 9000 years—give or take 80. (Old boots and shoes found date from a later period.)

If you turn on Stravinsky's *Rite of Spring* in your head and wander slowly along the paths, the life-size models of beasts scattered throughout the park may seem to come to life. At the least, you can watch bubbles rise from the primordial ooze, and at one observation pit you can examine a tangle of fossilized bones left stuck in the muck just as they were found.

Others, assembled in skeletons, fill the whole Hancock Hall at the Natural History Museum in Exposition Park (see Chapter 3). It's a spookier place, but moving, and with the tar pits form the first steps on the trail of Los Angeles' history.

Southwest Museum

SOUTHWEST MUSEUM

The first Angelenos lived only eight miles east of the La Brea tar pits in the village of Yang-na. Like the other small Indian tribes of Southern California, this group of Gabrielenos were a peaceful folk living in harmony with their environment. Their homes were rounded thatch huts like those seen in the historical section of the State and County Arboretum in Arcadia. They relied on acorns and small game for food, and drank the waters of what is now the concrete-jacketed Los Angeles River. Some met and mixed with Cabrillo's party in 1542, and their descendants traded with the company of Portolá who camped near Yang-na in 1769 on the first overland exploration in Southern California.

You can't show your visitors Yang-na. It became one of California's first "ghost towns." The village site lies somewhere in the heart of downtown, possibly under the present City Hall. But you can take your guests to the Southwest Museum, on Museum Drive off the Pasadena Freeway via Ave. 43. Here is one of the finest collections of Indian artifacts in the Southwest, with special halls for California Indians, Plains Indians, Southwest ethnology, basketry and prehistory. Boys will love the tepee, spears and feathered headresses; girls the dolls, beaded moccasins and miniature baskets. (Other Indian artifacts are displayed on the lower floors of the Natural History Museum and at the Antelope Valley Indian Museum in Lancaster.)

After visiting the Southwest Museum, stop also at Casa de Adobe on N. Figueroa, and at El Alisal, the hand-built home of Charles Lummis, founder of the museum. Both are nearby.

THE OLD MISSIONS

Soon after the arrival of Spanish padres, many of the Yang-na villagers and other Indians who peopled Southern Califor-

67

San Gabriel Mission

nia found themselves attached to one of the 21 Franciscan missions established between 1769 and 1823 by Junípero Serra and his successors. Founded to convert Indians to Christianity and bring European culture to an aboriginal wilderness, the missions also became vast economic holdings—with farms, vineyards, cattle ranches, tanneries and the like. The main buildings (the only visible remains of the Church's dominion) were eventually located about a day's journey apart from San Diego to Monterey and connected by El Camino Real, The King's Highway—known in the 1960's as the Hippie Highway.

Touring the missions was a must in pre-Disneyland days, and even now some visitors "collect" missions as some inter-continental travelers "collect" countries. Perhaps even more than before, the missions offer a refreshing change from the usual tourist itinerary, and their architectural, cultural and spiritual significance make them worthy of more than a casual visit.

San Gabriel Archángel, located a few miles north of the San Bernardino Freeway in San Gabriel, is the more interesting of the two missions in Los Angeles. On Sunday you can listen to Mass in the huge Moorish structure which dates from 1791. Museum exhibits include original Indian paintings of the stations of the cross, books that date back to 1489 and a photograph of Robert Kennedy who visited the mission two weeks before his assassination. Be sure to descend into the cool, musty sacristy —the best preserved part of the building. Here you will see a massive chest covered with an original hide bearing the cattle brand of the mission—one of the wealthiest. You will also see a large circular mirror—the convex kind you find in dime stores and supermarkets today. "Notice the mirror on the wall," a sign reads. "It was used by the padres during Mass to watch the movements of the Indians." A good clue that the neophytes were as much utilized as catechized.

Pico House, Los Angeles Plaza

Of the other missions nearby, Mission San Fernando (also within L.A. city limits) is rich in relics and has a beautiful garden. To the south, San Juan Capistrano is much restored from earthquake damage but suffers greatly from the surrounding touristy atmosphere. Northward, Mission Santa Inés in Solvang boasts one of the finest collections of art treasures, and Mission Santa Barbara is widely praised for its classical beauty and decorative arts. But the loveliest mission by far is La Purísima, near Lompoc. Operated as a state historic park, the buildings and surrounding 960 acres have been faithfully reconstructed and redeveloped to approximate the setting you would have found in the early 1800's.

OLD PLAZA AREA

Ten years after Mission San Gabriel was founded in 1771 as the first outpost of "civilization" in the Los Angeles basin, the city of Nuestra Señora La Reina de Los Angeles de Porciúncula (now simply L.A.) had its inauspicious beginning. On the evening of September 4, 1781, the Indians of Yang-na watched 44 weary travelers settle on a site preselected for its farming potential by Felipe de Neve, California's Spanish governor.

Amazingly enough, you and your historic-minded guests can see that birthplace today—just across the Santa Ana Freeway from the modern Civic Center. Visiting the Old Plaza area (which is protected and managed as an historic park) can be a frightful drag or full of exciting discoveries—depending on how you approach it.

The best way is to join one of the docent tours (usually given Tuesday through Saturday). Instead of reading dull notes about old landmarks, you may get a lovely young guide who can bring the dead to life and flesh out the empty buildings. First she should confess that Los Angeles was a rough town where gam-

71

bling, drinking and violence were as much a part of its style as fiestas and holy processions. There were daily murders in the 1850's; Indians were often sold into virtual slavery as late as 1869; and in 1871 about 20 Chinese were massacred here.

She may also explain that the original plaza was first a barren square, beaten hard by the crossings of farmers and ranchers with their horses, cattle, carretas and bulls and bears—the latter often pitted against each other for entertainment. The bandstand, she'll note, is new. But when Commodore Stockton entered the pueblo in 1847 to claim it for the Union, he had his band play on this spot. So well, in fact, that the deserted plaza soon filled with cheering Angelenos.

Your guide will also lead you down Olvera Street (see Chapter 5), pointing out the 1818 Ávila adobe and other early buildings, and describing how the first residents threw their trash on the street where tourists now stroll. She can show you the Pico House, the first three-story structure in Los Angeles. The once elegant hotel was built in 1870 by Pio Pico, the last Mexican governor of California, before he lost all his ranchos and went flat broke.

Highlight of the tour, however, is the Old Plaza Church—partly financed by the sale of brandy donated by the mission, and dedicated in 1822. Though restored and redecorated many times, it does contain some original walls. Come to Los Angeles' mother church on Saturday—wedding day, baptism day. You'll find the gaiety and high hopes of the young Mexican-American couples that fill the church yard rubbing off on you. Here past, present and future can conjoin in a memorable moment.

A SAMPLING OF OTHER HISTORIC PLACES

The Old Plaza area is the only place in Los Angeles where you may conveniently show your guests reminders of the city's history from its earliest days as a quiet farming pueblo, its bustling years as a town center during the much-romanticized "days of the dons," all the way to the turn of the century when its dominant Spanish-Mexican culture faded beneath the onrush of Midwestern and Eastern settlers and Los Angeles became a modern, distinctly North-American urban metropolis.

If your guests ask for another excursion into the past, you can take them to the Los Angeles State and County Arboretum in Arcadia. Within the 127-acre botanical park are the Hugo Reid House (a restored three-room adobe dating from 1839, home of the original owner of Rancho Santa Anita and the most authentic example of a typical small early-California ranch house); Queen Anne Cottage (the 1881 gingerbread Victorian home of E. J. "Lucky" Baldwin, a Comstock-lode millionaire who purchased the rancho in 1874 for $200,000); a richly appointed Coach Barn; and a freshly reconstructed Santa Fe depot (moved to the Arboretum in 1969 when the Foothill Freeway demanded its original site).

From here on, a systematic pursuit of the past becomes difficult. Other adobes and early residences dot the area, though many are so completely surrounded by modern features that it requires special talents to recapture a feeling for their place in time. The reconstructed Pio Pico house in Whittier, the 1864 Phineas Banning residence in Wilmington and the Leonis Adobe in Calabasas are worthy of visits.

So, too, is Fort Tejon, found some 66 miles north of Los Angeles in the Tehachapi Mountains near Gorman. Home of the U.S. Cavalry's First Dragoons between 1854 and 1864, the fort was also a stopping place for the Butterfield Overland Mail and briefly the base for Colonel Beale's famous camel corps. Now nicely restored and operated as a state historic park, the tranquil fort area is open daily. Peace is broken, however, on the third

Los Angeles State and County Arboretum

Sunday of each month (except December through February). That's when costumed Blues and Grays line up with muskets, hand guns and cannon and fight it out till the last man is down —reenacting events that never took place at Fort Tejon.

Historical landmarks are sometimes alive. Among the 100 historic-cultural monuments so designated by the Los Angeles Cultural Heritage Board are two notable trees—the Moreton Bay Fig Tree (an 1875 goliath with a 120-foot span, at 11000 National Blvd.) and the Encino Oak (estimated to be 1000 years old, found on Louise Avenue, 210 feet south of Ventura Boulevard).

While the past can pop up in strange shapes and places, one especially rich lode of history is concentrated in the Saugus-Newhall area north of the San Fernando Valley—and not far from the epicenter of the 1971 earthquake. Until the Ridge Route was opened in this century, Fremont Pass (now slashed by the Antelope Valley Freeway) was *the* overland northern route into and out of Los Angeles. The first big oil fields discovered in California were also tapped in Newhall, and you can still see the 1876 Pioneer Oil Refinery structure in the city. Not far from it is William S. Hart Park. The famed cowboy star of the silent screen donated his estate to the county, which maintains a rather good Old West museum in the Hart house. Within the 220-acre park are many fine picnic spots.

Another pleasant Newhall site for a picnic outing is Placerita Canyon Park. Here, in 1842 while on a lunch break of his own, Francisco Lopez pulled up a wild onion to find bright gold particles hanging from the roots. It was the first major discovery of gold in California, one that yielded about $10,000 that year. But no great cause for anything but local excitement. The big strike was to come six years later when James Marshall tapped the Mother Lode at Sutter's Mill.

Huntington Library

Marshall's find brought adventurers from all over the world rushing to the Golden State, many of whom soon abandoned the northern frenzy and headed south for Los Angeles. Others struck it rich and some of them took to *importing* history and culture.

One of the better legacies left by the new breed of Yankee millionaires can be seen at the Huntington Library, Art Gallery and Botanical Gardens. In case you don't know, Henry E. Huntington was the man who gave Los Angeles its first and only rapid transit system. Nephew of Collis P. Huntington, who brought the Southern Pacific Railroad to the city, H.E. consolidated and expanded a network of trolleys (the Pacific Electric Railway's Big Red Cars) that crisscrossed the L.A. basin for 40 years.

Henry was a lucky guy. A wealthy man in his own right, he inherited a bundle from Collis in 1900. Then in 1913, he married Arabella, his late uncle's wife. Together they collected rare books and art works and had exquisite gardens planted on their San Marino estate.

Henry was also generous. In 1919 he put the world-famous collections in trust for the people, and in 1928 the estate was opened free to the public. On view in the library is a Gutenberg *Bible,* the Ellesmere manuscript of Chaucer's *Canterbury Tales* and a page from Benjamin Franklin's *Autobiography* written in his own hand. The art gallery, once the Huntingtons' home, has Lawrence's *Pinkie,* Gainsborough's *The Blue Boy* and a wealth of 18th-century French and British arts and furnishings. The grounds include a Japanese garden, a Shakespeare garden, plus sections for cacti, roses, herbs, camellias, azaleas, palms, oranges and avocados. (H. E. used to take avocado seeds home from the Jonathan Club, and the San Marino grove is recognized as the first commercial avocado growth in California.)

77

Happily, much of the former stuffiness has disappeared from the Huntington. And though it's still not recommended for fidgety preschoolers, guests with a bent for scholarship, fine arts and gardens will find a visit here a special treat. (Closed Mondays and all of October.)

5 ETHNIC ADVENTURES

Los Angeles was first inhabited by Indians, first "discovered" by Spaniards and first settled by 44 *pobladores,* among whom were Spaniards, Negroes, Indians and mestizos. Since then it has become home to Greeks, Yugoslavs, Portuguese, Filipinos and other immigrants from all over the world. But it is not a cosmopolitan city like San Francisco. Nor is it the melting pot New York is.

To be sure, Los Angeles has a large Negro ghetto and an equally sizable chicano barrio. There is a Chinese enclave downtown and a Jewish gathering place along Fairfax Boulevard north of Farmers Market. Yet, Angel Town is basically a WASP town. Most citizens migrated here all the way from, say, Iowa—or Indiana or Oklahoma. The Europeans who came did so in small groups—usually from other American cities—and have been absorbed into the dominant culture. Our largest Oriental minority, the Japanese, dispersed all over the city after World War II and are now living like their WASP neighbors in suburbs like Gardena, Monterey Park and West Los Angeles.

So if you ask a typical Los Angeles resident his idea of an ethnic adventure and he says strolling down Olvera Street on a Sunday afternoon or having dinner at a Polynesian restaurant, don't assume he's an Archie Bunker. Assimilation is simply a fact in Los Angeles, as it is in probably no other large American city. And yet, there are a few spots where you and your guests may sample the exotic and get a glimpse into our ethnic heritage.

Olvera Street

INDIAN POWWOWS

A frighteningly large number of children grow up thinking the only Indians in Los Angeles are on their TV screens, fighting losing battles with men in blue coats. The 1970 census reports that 24,509 American Indians live in Los Angeles County alone, although the true figure runs closer to 60,000 according to the Los Angeles Indian Center—which ought to know. Why the difference? "The census is wrong," a Center worker explains. "Indians are very transient, and they just aren't where census takers are."

Where Indians are, many times, is at Indian bars—one of the first places the Indian Center directs new arrivals to the city. If your visitors want to see Indians in Southern California—but not at bars—consider attending one of the monthly powwows sponsored by groups like the Little Big Horn Indian Association, Many Trails Indian Club and the American Indian Tribal Dancers. Outsiders are welcome at these powwows—usually held at community centers—and can view dancing and traditional ceremonials, meet and mix with Indians as neighbors.

The Los Angeles Indian Center on S. New Hampshire has up-to-date information on these and other activities open to visitors. And for locations of Indian-owned craft shops and restaurants, contact the Urban Indian Development Assn. on Wilshire Boulevard.

OLVERA STREET

Visitors who have never been south of Tijuana or Juarez and are seeking a taste of Old Mexico usually find Olvera Street enchanting. Once in the heart of Los Angeles when it was an outpost of Spain, and then Mexico, the block-long avenue is a happy mixture of historical buildings, Mexican eateries, craftsmen's shops and *puestos*—little stalls where you can pick up inexpensive souvenirs made in the U.S. and Taiwan, some even in Mexico.

Located downtown between the Old Plaza area (see Chapter 4) and Macy Street, Olvera Street is a 20th-century recreation of an early Mexican marketplace—and a cheerful spot to spend an hour or more, especially on Saturday or Sunday. At the La Golondrina restaurant, for example, you can see tortillas being made by hand, enjoy mariachi music and flamenco dancing in the evening, or sit outside with a *cerveza* and *taco* and watch the tourists stroll by. The restaurant, incidentally, occupies the former wine cellar of the 1855 Pelanconi House, and across the street is the 1818 Avila Adobe, Los Angeles' earliest remaining residence. At the north end of the block, on an exterior wall of Italian Hall, you may see the faint remains of a fresco by famed Mexican muralist David Alfaro Siqueiros. Titled *Tropical America,* it shocked and angered anti-revolutionary gringos in 1932 and has since been abandoned to the elements.

At Christmas time Olvera Street takes on a particularly festive air. For about a week there are nightly candlelight processions where the old songs of *Las Posadas* are sung in Spanish. Take the kids along; they might get a chance to break a *piñata* afterwards. And you may find that here Christmas takes on a meaning it once had.

EL MERCADO

While the average visitor is satisfied with Olvera Street, truly *simpatico turistas* may prefer to visit El Mercado—a two-story galleria of shops built in 1968 by and for the contemporary Mexican-American community. That community, by the way, is *muy grande*. Exact figures are hard to come by, though it is often said Los Angeles has the largest number of Mexicans on the North American continent outside of Mexico City. And most live in East Los Angeles, not very far from El Mercado.

Here families come, usually on Saturday and Sunday, to market in the central grocery store, at the butcher shop with its lambs' heads and pig snouts, at record and magazine stalls, at wig shops and spice counters. You can descend to the basement and survey the going bargains. Or climb to the second story and survey *la raza*. If you sit at a small table overlooking the first floor, enjoying an Orange Crush and a snack from one of the numerous food stalls, you'll hear the lilting tones of Spanish instead of English and the stirring strains of Mexican soul music instead of Muzak.

You can find El Mercado on East First Street near Cheesbrough, a few blocks off the Pomona Freeway.

LITTLE TOKYO

If you drive too fast along First Street, just east of City Hall, you'll probably miss Little Tokyo. This tiny area centered at First and San Pedro is the cultural, spiritual and commercial home for over 100,000 Japanese-Americans—the largest Japanese community in the continental United States. (Before World War II, of course, it was also a residential home—emptied when Executive Order 9066 uprooted an entire people and relocated them in detention camps.)

Japanese Town, as the Japanese call it, is old, unprepossessing and somewhat run-down, though the Little Tokyo Redevelopment Project forsees a sparkling new center in the near future. The time to come is on Sunday, when parking is easier to find. Take slowly to the streets and you may experience a real treat. Like hearing a chanting of a *sutra* in Koyasan Buddhist Temple, hidden at the end of a narrow alleyway off First Street. Or discovering a miniature garden in front of the Merit Savings & Loan. Or sampling some *tempura* or *sushi* (raw fish) at the Ka-

Chinatown

wafuku or Tokyo Kaikan restaurants. Or seeing a kimono-clad mother buying sweets for her doll-like children. If you're lucky, you may even get to witness an impromptu parade by the Commodore Perry Boy Scout troop.

The big parade, complete with schools of *ondo* dancing girls, comes each August as a climax to the annual Nisei Week Festival—the only time Little Tokyo deliberately puts on a show.

Japanese Town is a place that grows on you. The more often you return, the more you discover what you missed the last time.

CHINATOWN

Across the Hollywood Freeway and not far from Little Tokyo, Chinatown is altogether another cup of tea. Huge gateways facing the 900 blocks of N. Broadway and Hill let you know right away that this show is mostly for tourists. They walk over from Olvera Street, wearing sombreros and carrying *piñatas,* ready now to toss a coin into a wishing well, have their handwriting analyzed by an IBM machine or buy a Mao jacket. "Sure we get Mao jackets," a lady at the Hong Kong shop says. "But not from *Red* China. We get from Japan—much cheaper!"

Guests who have visited San Francisco's Chinatown will find the activities along Gin Ling Way disappointing. One thing missing are the poultry and grocery shops with all their incredible aromas. And unless you come at lunchtime, you may not see many Chinese. Los Angeles is home to over 40,000 Chinese-Americans and most live within a five-mile radius of Chinatown. (Walls in the area, adorned with Chinese ideographs from that curse of our time—the spray-paint can—point up that fact.) But they shop down around N. Spring, near Macy and Ord, especially in the early evening and on Sundays.

Still, Chinatown can be fun, particularly for visitors whose only view of the Orient is from an Alan Ladd flick. Good Cantonese food is available—at restaurants like George Lim's, New Hung Far, the Golden Pagoda and General Lee's—as well as others less well-known. And among the curio shops are fine-art emporiums like Far East Imports where discriminating buyers can find rare and expensive silk screens, jades, coral, ivory and lacquerware.

If your guests are with you in late January or early February, take them to the Chinese New Year celebration. There'll be fire-crackers, dragons and whoop-de-do. And you'll all have a *Gung Hay Fat Choy!*

6 THE MAGNETIC COAST

Land's end for some 1000 magnificent miles, California offers one continuous confrontation with the awesome and not always pacific Pacific. It's a varied coast of bays and estuaries, rocky headlands and rolling dunes, hidden coves and long, white-sanded beaches (most of them confined to the southern third of the state from Santa Barbara to San Diego).

Whether native or newcomer, the Southern Californian soon finds the sea in his blood. Take him too far or too long from the scent of tidewater and he gets to feeling itchy. Be he a bather or worshipper of sand and sun, a dock-walker or pier habitué, a waterskier or skin-diver, a surfer or hodad, a sailor who finds freedom at the end of a tiller or a fisherman who takes his ease with pole in hand, time and again he turns to the Pacific for sustenance and solace.

Ninety percent of California's population lives within one hour of the coast. And if you've ever tried to get to it on a summer weekend, you'd have sworn all 90 percent were there. (You'd also know it took them considerably more than one hour to drive the clogged roads west.) Such is the siren call of the maternal brine that each year some 60 million people visit the beaches in Los Angeles County alone—more visits by far than to any other recreational attraction in all of California—man-made or otherwise.

All this people pressure has had its unkind results. While everything below the mean high tide line legally belongs to the people, about half of L.A. County's coastline is in private hands. Houses, apartments, power plants, sewage-treatment facilities,

Palisades Park, Santa Monica

oil refineries and drilling rigs, billboards, greasy spoons and other effluents of civilization often block the sea view and leave much of the coast inaccessible. Too many thoughtless visitors ignore trash cans and deposit their waste on the shore. Others, including supposedly supervised school science classes, have so thoroughly stripped our tidepools of sea life a state law had to be enacted in 1972 prohibiting the removal of anything from the pools—dead or alive. Even some of our most appealing beach areas (like the Manhattan-Hermosa-Redondo stretch and Malibu's Coral and Surfrider beaches) have such limited parking facilities that it's almost impossible to get near them on a summer weekend.

Withal, the Pacific has priceless amenities, and even standing on a high bluff overlooking the endless blue expanse can be a restorative. So if your guests are inlanders or have salt in their veins, by all means take them to the biggest and bluest ocean.

A few reminders and suggestions: The water is brought to us courtesy of the Japanese current; coming by way of the Aleutians, it can be bone-chilling even under a 90-degree sun. And the sun often acts like it's over the Sahara; fair-skinned visitors unaccustomed to its special rays may find themselves painfully burned in 20 minutes, even under a misty sky. If you must do your sea thing on the same day as everyone else, try to get there by 10 in the morning or after 4 p.m. For elbow room on those days, head for one of the newer or bigger beaches (like Zuma, Leo Carrillo and Point Mugu in the north; Huntington or Doheny in the south)—even if you have to drive farther.

For a scenic drive there's nothing to match the Palos Verdes Peninsula. Start northward on Gaffey Street from the tip of Point Fermin in San Pedro, stopping at the circular turnout across from Fort MacArthur for an overview of the harbor. Then turn west on 25th (which merges into Palos Verdes

Drive) and continue around the bright peninsula to Torrance.

To see surfers catching a curl or attaching sails to their boards and riding the wind, go to Malibu Surfrider, Manhattan, Hermosa or Redondo beach piers, or to Huntington Beach. For an old-fashioned wienie-roast, there's Playa del Rey's Dockweiler Beach. It's directly under L.A. International's take-off flight path, but the beach is wide, clean, little-used and has fire rings.

Those leery of the surf should stay near a manned lifeguard station or go to either Cabrillo Beach (which faces *east*) or to Long Beach (also behind the breakwater, the sea is so calm here lifeguards chuckle over its big "six-inch breakers"). And for a complete getaway, Catalina Island still lies 26 miles offshore and can be reached year-round by boat or plane from terminals in San Pedro.

BEACHES

To most visitors the sea means the beach, and Southern California has more good, *usable* beaches than any other part of the country. Every resident has his favorite (and it's not necessarily the closest to home), but for sheer beauty, a few stand out above the others:

(1) La Jolla. With lots of grassy spaces, palms, pines and benches nearby, northern San Diego's "jewel city" has a long shores area, a famous cove, and Wind 'N' Sea—a beach as fetching as its name.

(2) Laguna Beach. A self-styled art colony and home of the annual summer Pageant of the Masters (where citizens present living recreations of famous paintings), Laguna boasts lovely beaches backed by rugged cliffs, rocks to climb on and even a few tidepools. It's fun to stroll around town, too.

(3) Newport-Balboa. The beaches aren't especially good, but the setting, with islands and yachts, is perfectly picturesque.

Back in Los Angeles there are more fine beaches—each with its own character and characters. To mention only a few, let's start with the one that tops the character list—Venice.

Developed in the 1900's as a resort town set around a network of man-made canals (with imported gondoliers, carnivals, dance halls and the whole joyful bit), and later the starting place of the beat movement (the original one), Venice has fallen on strange and transitional days. Right next to each other you can find a tidy old shingle house where some proper old lady lives out her last years; a run-down old shingle house surrounded by trash and adorned with hip-art; a pasteboard apartment inhabited by an interracial family of counter-culture persuasion; and a slick new expensive apartment house with self-cleaning ovens in the kitchens and Porsches in the carports. You can see all this—as well as occasional glimpses of the sloughy fenced-off remains of the Grand Canal—driving south along Pacific Ave. toward Via Marina, which takes you right into Marina del Rey and a completely different scene. Venice also has a good beach and a new concrete fishing pier, but your visitors may very well say, "Drive on!"

North of Venice, beginning just past Pacific Ocean Pier where the remains of a defunct amusement park present a ghostly scene, is Santa Monica. Sitting almost in the middle of the great Santa Monica Bay, this city was nearly selected as the site of L.A.'s port. Spared that dubious fate, Santa Monica offers sweeping vistas encompassing Palos Verdes on the south and Malibu on the north—providing it's a clear day. From Palisades Park, a narrow bluff-top strip running about one and a half miles from Colorado to San Vicente, you can look out over noisy Pacific Coast Highway, celebrities' homes, a broad public beach and on to the sea. (Behind you is high-rise—more and more of it.) At the southern end of Santa Monica, from Pacific

Point Fermin

Ocean Pier to Bay Street is another excellent beach. Recently tidied up, and with new parking additions, it's a favorite for families—and youths in summer. For color and character(s), however, the place to go is the pier and the beach immediately to the south. In these two places you can show your guests everything they wanted (or didn't want) to see in Los Angeles—fishermen and fisherkids; sit-down seafood restaurants and dog-on-a-stick snack bars; tiny tots playing tag in the nude and old codgers in dark suits playing checkers; clean-cut All-American girls and spaced-out kids sleeping it off on the sand. There's a charming old merry-go-round on the pier, while several blocks south Synanon (the self-help half-way house for narcotic addicts) occupies the exclusive old Del Mar Club. Just eastward, between Ocean and Main, you can show your guests The RAND Corporation, the "think tank" of Herman Kahn and Daniel Ellsburg fame.

Northwestward from Santa Monica is Malibu, or *The* Malibu as insiders call it. Home to movie stars and meeting place for surfers, Malibu has received much ballyhoo. Today, however, the stars have lost some of their shine, and the golden sun gods have slipped in the cult department. (Easy-rider bike folk seem to have momentarily taken their transitory place in our pantheon of pop heros.) At Malibu you can show your guests the best and worst of Southern California's coast. The worst is found east of the Sea Lion restaurant — a chain of utility poles and "houses" that look like shoe boxes on stilts, so ugly that if they were transplanted to most slums they'd be considered the blight of the neighborhood. (A two-bedroom place may go for about $1500 a month in summer.) The best is a beautiful drive along Pacific Coast Highway west from Malibu Canyon Rd., and some of the finest beaches around: Paradise Cove (a private beach with fishing pier), new Point Dume State Beach (via

Ports O' Call

Westward), Pirate's Cove (south over the rocks from Point Dume, unlifeguarded and sometimes a nudist hideaway), Zuma (a huge beach with excellent facilities) and Leo Carrillo (one of the least used).

Some of the wind has lately been taken out of Malibu's sails by the South Bay beaches—Torrance, Redondo, Hermosa and Manhattan. Residents brag about the Esplanade, a beachside drive that locals call (not very accurately) "the Riviera of the West." Then, too, these sands are supposedly where the swinging singles gather—stewardesses, interns, young attorneys and other relatively well-heeled fun-loving types. Since apartments hug the coast here (one actually jutting out to the mean high tide line), parking is limited, though there is a new multi-level parking structure at the base of the Redondo Beach Pier. The pier, by the way, is short on self-conscious cuteness, long on native color, and well worth a visit if you're in the area. At the entrance you can buy fresh shrimp cocktails or other sea meats, and at pier's end you can eavesdrop among authentic old salts and fish wives. Connected to the fishing pier is another, semicircular pier with gift shops, restaurants, snack bars and views of bathers, surfers and weekend sailors out of the nearby King Harbor Marina.

PORT OF LOS ANGELES

In the 1880's the short-sighted New York *Tribune* said Los Angeles "can never be a great business center because it is too far from the ocean." But Los Angeles has never let a mere matter like distance (or lack of fresh water, or earthquakes) impede its progress. In the 1890's it began developing the mudflats of San Pedro Bay into what is now the largest man-made harbor in the western hemisphere and the west coast's leading port in cargo tonnage. (It also annexed San Pedro, which lies about 23

95

miles southwest of downtown, and a "shoe-string strip" of territory to connect the two.)

If your guests like dockside scenes—freighters, luxury liners, fishing boats, tuna canneries, super-automated container terminals and scrap heaps—plan an afternoon at the Port of Los Angeles. Down at the end of the Harbor Freeway, the port covers 7000 acres of land and water, encompasses three major districts (Wilmington, San Pedro and Terminal Island) and rubs shoulders with the adjacent Port of Long Beach. Since the area is vast, take along a good map or write the port for a free tour booklet.

The main visitor attraction is Ports O' Call and Whaler's Wharf, situated on the west side of the main channel (and well-marked from the freeway's end). With tree-shaded cobblestone walkways, restaurants and snack bars, over 70 individual shops, several choices of harbor excursion facilities and good lookout points across the channel, Ports O' Call is a pleasant, albeit touristy, spot to sniff the salt.

Until recently some visitors found the approach through San Pedro's notorious Beacon Street skid-row district more than a little unsettling. But urban renewal has come to San Pedro, and only a few bars, pawn shops and 25-cent peep shows remain. Where have the "bums" gone? "I guess most go to Long Beach," a long-time resident said. "At least there they can still be by the water."

Allow time to take the green Vincent Thomas suspension toll bridge that arches over to Terminal Island. You won't find any picturesque palms waving above pseudo-Polynesian restaurants here, but down by the canneries you may notice Joe Biff's saloon advertising "beer time mates." And do drive by berths 210 and 211 to show your guests an instructive example of recycling. Here the Hugo Neu Proler Corporation's machines take stripped and flattened cast-off cars and chew them up into fist-size shreds of "macaroni." Shipped to Japan for refashioning, some of the metal returns to Los Angeles (at berths 134 and 135) in the form of new Datsuns.

MARINA DEL REY

Another mudflat turned harbor, Marina del Rey is the world's largest man-made parking lot for small pleasure craft. Besides accommodating 6000 boats (at the rate of $2 per foot per month), it also houses some 10,000 residents (whose apartments go at the rate of $200 to $1850 per month). At these prices, and with pitifully few parking places for casual sightseers, the marina is indeed a very private club. One lure for outsiders is the 40-shop, 3-restaurant Fisherman's Village—an imitation Cape Cod on concrete found on the east side of the main channel at the end of Fiji Way. Here you can watch sailors, rent a boat or board a harbor excursion. But it's much more fun to drive to the western end of Via Marina (if you can find a parking spot), sit on the rocks bordering the entrance channel and watch the dinghies tack their way out to sea while the larger auxiliaries and the "stinkpots" motor close aboard.

DINING BY THE WATER

Known as a city of gourmands rather than gourmets, Los Angeles has many good but relatively few really fine restaurants, and nowhere is this more evident than along the coast. Even so, there are unforgettable pleasures in dining on or near the water, and you can do your guests and yourself a favor by planning a lunch or dinner at one of the following selected restaurants. (As usual, recommendations are cautionary and reservations are advised. And do specify a window table if you want the best possible view.)

97

Marina Del Rey

To be surfside: The Sea Lion (on the Malibu Coast) or Jack's at the Beach (on Ocean Park Pier in Santa Monica). For marina scenes: The Warehouse (at Marina del Rey), Donkin's Inn (a singles gathering place, also at Marina del Rey), or The Stuft Shirt (on the bay at Newport Beach). To overlook the sea: Le Monaco (on a bluff in Palos Verdes Estates), The Victor Hugo Inn (cliffside in Laguna Beach), or the Quiet Cannon (high above the harbor at Dana Point). For harbor sights: *SS Princess Louise* (tied up at Terminal Island across from Ports O' Call) or *Reuben E. Lee* (docked at the eastern end of San Diego's Harbor Island).

Balboa Park, San Diego

7 ESCAPE SOUTH

Where do Angelenos go to get away from it all? To Las Vegas if they want a gawdy-bawdy whirl of nonstop razzmatazz and a flirtation with possible financial disaster. To Palm Springs if they really want to unwind, breathe clean dry air and bake in the sun. But often as not, their escape to fun *and* sun is San Diego—the year-round playground that *Ladies Home Journal* once named the "most livable city" in the nation and San Diego writer Neil Morgan called "a kind of sunny patio" for Los Angeles and all the Southwest.

Until recently, though, Angelenos saw their southern neighbor as a provincial backwater, a safe but essentially unexciting cul-de-sac off the mainroad of civilization. Visitors making the trek south from L.A. also frequently got bogged down in crowded beach towns. When they finally emerged through the Rose Canyon gateway to San Diego they literally had to hold their noses as miles of unsightly marshes and mudflats greeted them with a stench of decaying marine life and trash.

All that has changed. Rocked by more than one major political scandal, San Diego has *almost* overcome its image as a haven for retired admirals and geranium-potting conservatives. As for getting there, Interstate 5 is now a brisk, often scenic two-hour drive slicing through coast towns like San Clemente (of Richard Nixon fame), Oceanside (which has a nice little harbor) and Del Mar (where horses run in summer), and bypassing old "slaughter alley"—a dangerous stretch of Highway 101 near San Onofre that used to help keep the population in check. And from those mudflats has blossomed Mission Bay Aquatic Park, a

San Diego Zoo

4600-acre pleasure ground partly planted to grass and palm trees. Polynesian-style hostelries (like Vacation Village) and restaurants (like the Bahia) dot the still-developing park where sailors, waterskiers, anglers and bathers do their thing around 27 miles of shoreline.

In fact, many visitors now never make it past Mission Bay into San Diego proper. For here, too, is Sea World—one of the city's newest family attractions and, some say, "the best show in town." (See Chapter 1.)

But there is much more to show your guests in San Diego, and this chapter touches only a few highlights. Whether you have one brief day or as many as five, there will always be something new worth discovering—like Torrey Pines State Park, Scripps Institution of Oceanography and the La Jolla Museum of Contemporary Art. One warning for first-time visitors: San Diego has subtle but persuasive charms. Many of its nearly one million residents first came as tourists and found themselves hurrying back to stay forever.

BALBOA PARK

San Diegans like to tell you that "the park came first, then we built the city around it." Though it's not quite true it's true enough. While California's first city was founded in 1769, only 2301 residents called it home in 1868 when the 1400-acre park was created. And even if it remained mostly in native chaparral for many decades, the park is still a marvelous lesson in priorities for future city planners. The ready availability of well-maintained picnic areas, gardens, museums, playgrounds and other cultural and recreational facilities may help to explain why San Diegans seem a little saner than folks from Los Angeles. At any rate, locals are justly proud of their park, and out-of-towners are lucky to be able to share it.

You and your guests could easily spend an entire day along Laurel Boulevard, the park's main cross street. Here is the highly respected Fine Arts Gallery, a fun place which has "something for everyone," according to its director. Next to it the tiny, exquisite (if sometimes uppity) Timken Art Gallery boasts exceptional works of Italian, Flemish and Spanish masters along with a room of Russian icons. Nearby are the Museum of Man, the Natural History Museum, a new planetarium and space science center, the Cassius Carter Center Stage theater and the Old Globe (home of the annual summer National Shakespeare Festival). Just strolling along the eucalyptus-shaded avenue, gazing at the Spanish-renaissance architecture and pausing at the reflecting pool, is free therapy.

SAN DIEGO ZOO

Smack in the heart of Balboa Park is the internationally famous San Diego Zoo—still the city's odds-on favorite tourist destination and the best buy in town. More than three million people pass through its turnstiles each year to view the world's largest collection of wild animals. Over 5500 healthy specimens of about 1600 species are displayed here—most of them uncaged and separated from spectators only by moats.

Some visitors head straight for the much-imitated but unequaled children's zoo to reestablish contact with their furry or feathered friends. For others the animals seem an incidental side show for the main attraction—the greenery. As much a botanical garden as a zoological garden, the zoo's trees, shrubs, ferns and flowering plants are valued at no less then $35 million and represent a greater investment than do the animals.

Still, it's the beasts that come first—everything from aardvarks to zebras, noble manlike great apes to strange prehistoric kiwis. To see them, you can strike out on your own over the 128

104

acres of mesas and canyons, utilizing moving sidewalks, escalators or the gondola-car Skyfari. But the best beginning is the 40-minute guided bus tour which covers about 80 percent of the park. (The rest you can comfortably do on foot.) The well-informed drivers present a running commentary that is often entertaining, and sometimes trenchant. Stopping before three polar bears splashing happily about their pool one driver noted "At the present kill rate, these bears won't outlast the century. So-called 'sportsmen' stalk them by helicopter so they can decorate their homes without even getting their feet cold." Before a Cape buffalo: "Some people think this is the most dangerous animal in Africa. They're wrong. It's man." And bringing it closer to home: "To your left you see the Pacific brown pelican, a vanishing specie. Egg failures are running about 70 to 80 percent due to the use of DDT. In the Gulf of California, for example, the youngest birds we can find are about four or five years old."

WILD ANIMAL PRESERVE

To help preserve vanishing species, to encourage reproduction of others that feel inhibited in traditional zoos, and to offer visitors the chance to see wild animals in a more natural setting, the San Diego Zoo opened a new wild animal park in May, 1972. Located in San Pasqual, about 30 miles northeast of San Diego, the 1800-acre preserve sits in a peaceful rural valley near the site where General Kearny's American forces suffered a bloody defeat in 1846 at the hands of an angry army of Californios.

Little warfare is likely here now. The initial population of some 500 animals—including Cape buffaloes, giraffes, zebras, lions, wildebeasts, hartebeasts, sable antelopes, topis, Masai ostriches and 20 rare white rhinos—have been separated by inconspicuous moats according to group compatibility. (In one

San Diego Bay

compatibility experiment a foolish 75-pound springbok boldly attacked a 4500-pound rhino! So you won't see those two species together.)

To observe the animals as they roam freely about the hills and gather at watering pools, visitors board open-air electric trains that quietly wind around the preserve at 12 miles per hour. (No overheated cars and no claustrophobia as at Lion Country Safari.) You get a guided tour on the one-hour, five-mile trip. And while chances for arm's-length views like those possible at Lion Country are slim, you can walk out along special trails to areas like Lion Canyon (say with a picnic lunch) and stay there till closing time.

Back at the entrance Nairobi Village features a huge ape enclosure, a monkey island, ponds for waterfowl, a petting zoo, children's play section, restaurants, snack bars and other amenities for those just back from safari.

As with all new developments of this kind, the preserve is still rather barren. The grounds have been seeded, over $100,000 is being spent on vegetation, and before long it will look great. But even now the park is an agreeable place where you might want to take your guests—perhaps as an excuse for seeing it yourself. Take State Highway 78 from U.S. 395, about a 45-minute drive from downtown San Diego. And remember, summers generally will be hot.

HARBOR EXCURSION

"A landlocked and very good harbor." That was Juan Rodriguez Cabrillo's pronouncement when he discovered San Diego Bay in 1542. And it's still a very good harbor—for the U.S. Navy, international freighters, commercial and sport fishermen, weekend sailors, and tourists. For a stunning overview of the bay and a matchless vista of the city's new highrise skyline, first

107

Old Town, San Diego

take your guests out to Cabrillo National Monument on the tip of Point Loma. Then return to the foot of Broadway and join one of the daily guided harbor excursions—one of the most delightful and instructive water tours offered in all of Southern California.

The smooth, scenic one-hour trip takes you by the *Star of India,* the oldest merchant vessel afloat. Launched in 1863 from the Isle of Man, the handsome 275-foot windjammer has been lovingly restored and turned into a fine maritime museum which is open daily at a modest price. You also pass docks where surprisingly large tuna clippers tie up to mend their nets and (later) by canneries where ships not impounded by Peru or Ecuador deposit their catch. Visible, too, are Harbor Island (with not one, but two ITT-Sheraton hotels), Shelter Island (another man-made spit where marinas, restaurants and resort hotels nestle in a pseudo-Polynesian setting), and North Island (where the concept of the aircraft carrier was first developed). Throughout the cruise, of course, are close-up views of destroyers, cruisers, aircraft carriers and other active Navy ships.

For a truly unique experience, however, take the two-hour excursion. One extension of this trip passes the Naval Fueling Station (once a coaling station), the Nuclear Submarine Pier (where you can usually see six to ten subs at dock) and Ballast Point (very possibly the site where Cabrillo made landfall). At the other end of the excursion you see freight piers, ship foundries, floating cement dry docks and, most memorably, the Navy's mothball fleet. A hush is likely to fall over the boat as passengers catch sight of this awesome graveyard. Here some 150 sealed ships, veterans of the Battle of Okinawa, Leyte Gulf and other historic sea engagements, are moored in ghostly silence, as dead in their way as the thousands of seamen who died manning them. Elsewhere in the city it may be easy to chuckle

Mission San Diego de Alcalá

at San Diego's penchant for flag-waving, at the number of Stars and Stripes one sees floating atop its buildings and hanging from the eaves of its modest bungalows. But not here.

OLD TOWN

San Diego has taken on such a modern look with new skyscrapers, freeways, sports palaces and flashy hotels that one shouldn't be surprised to learn it also has a *new* Old Town. Nor should one be shocked to discover that the birthplace of California's first city now lies in a crotch of land where two freeways (Interstate 5 and U.S. 80) meet in a high-level, high-speed interchange.

Before the dawn of steel and concrete, in 1769, Junípero Serra and Gaspar de Portolá led a ragged band of priests and soldiers to this plot. On the side of the bluff now called Presidio Hill they founded the state's first mission and presidio. And just below it a town grew up as the center of a flourishing hide and tallow trade and later as a busy whaling port.

In the 1850's Old Town fell into decline as the city shifted southward to its present downtown core. But in the 1960's, when San Diegans began preparing for their bicentennial celebration, they decided it was high time to spruce up the place. Much of it was declared a state historic park in 1968, the bogus sign calling the city's earliest remaining adobe "Ramona's Marriage Place" was pulled down, and the building was nicely restored, whitewashed and furnished with period pieces.

For a faint flavor of San Diego's early Hispanic days you can join one of the park's tours, though more extensive, inspired and informed tours are offered each Saturday afternoon by the Historical Shrine Foundation. (These meet at the restored 1857 Whaley House just up San Diego Avenue from the Old Town plaza.)

What gripes purists the most is Bazaar del Mundo. A recent addition to Old Town, just across Calhoun Street from the plaza, the marketplace includes about 15 shops featuring fine arts, handicrafts, international wares, fresh produce and a restaurant with an inviting outdoor patio. "There's absolutely nothing historic about it!" protested one member of the Historical Shrine Foundation. Yet the Mexican-colonial-style buildings are attractive. And even if the bazaar is an obvious tourist trap, it's a pleasant one to be caught in.

From Old Town you can drive up to Presidio Park and visit the Serra Museum which marks the place where the original Mission San Diego de Alcalá was dedicated. Although the present building went up in this century, some of the doorway tiles date from the mission period. Older folks may enjoy studying the historical exhibits, and kids can let off steam rolling over grassy mounds on a hill below the nearby Serra Cross. You might want to tell them the corrugated sod covers the walls of the city's first fort.

MISSION SAN DIEGO

As it turned out, Father Serra picked a poor spot for the mission. There was no tillable soil nearby, the Indians were unusually hostile, and the soldiers proved more of a nuisance than a help. So, in 1774, the mission was moved some five miles up Mission Valley to its present location. As missions go, this one is not very picturesque, though it does have a magnificent *campanario*. If you can be choosy, stop instead at Mission San Luis Rey de Francia. Situated on a hill overlooking a rural setting near Oceanside, "The King of the Missions" was one of the largest of the 21—both in physical size and in the number of its Indian converts. Here you can tour a museum, finely reconstructed buildings and stroll about the beautiful gardens.

112

TIJUANA

If your guests have never set foot outside the good old US of A and regret it, you may as well prepare to take them to Tijuana. (Unless, of course, they are easily offended by poverty, poorly patched potholes and honky-tonk bars.) Tijuana is no more Mexican than it is American. (Some think it's a combination of the worst of both cultures.) But it is foreign. And the sound of mariachi music, the smell of leather *huaraches* and straw sombreros, and the taste of tequila and chili-spiced foods can at least suggest one is in "Old Mexico."

Those making the 20-minute drive south from San Diego are never alone. When it comes to tourism, Paris, London and Rome take a back seat to Tijuana, "the most visited city in the world." Why do so many "run" across the border to T.J.? Some go just to tread on alien ground. Some go to get married, or divorced. Others drive their cars down for tuck-and-roll upholstery jobs, while they wait. Still others go looking for easy-to-find sin.

But Tijuana offers more than junky souvenir stands and sleazy night clubs. Between May and September you can play *aficionado* at the bullfights. (Don't make the mistake of booing either the matador or the bull.) For a spirited evening of entertainment, there's *jai-alai,* an ancient Basque sport that's exciting to watch whether you gamble or not. And, good news for race fans, the Caliente track, home of the famous Caliente 5-10, is open again. Thoroughbreds run on weekends, greyhounds chase a mechanical rabbit Wednesday through Sunday evenings, and the foreign book is open daily, paying track odds on all major U.S. tracks operating that day.

And then there's the shopping (duty-free up to $100). Two respectable La Jolla matrons who regularly trade in town sug-

113

Tijuana, Mexico

gest visitors park at Woolworth's on *Avenida Revolución,* the city's main street. From there to the *jai-alai fronton,* they say, you can find everything you might want: Inexpensive mementos to take back home. Or fine silver work, native folk arts, hand-made clothing, perfumes imported from France or cashmere sweaters from Scotland. Yes, you can get all this in T.J.—and a lot more that needn't be mentioned here.

Mount Wilson Skyline Park

8   HIGH PLACES AND DRY PLACES

Now and again, when the gods favor Los Angeles with a still, smogless day, Angelenos and their guests awaken to discover that the sprawling city lies in a raggedy nest of mountains. Close at hand, the Santa Monicas appear as gentle mounds, though two pinnacles do top 3000 feet. To the east, the rugged San Gabriels jut up abruptly from the urban plain—great purple giants whose mile-and-a-half-high peaks can seem as threatening as inviting. And beyond these, from Ventura and Kern counties to the San Diego back country, from the Tehachapis to the Lagunas, are at least seven other major ranges taking in four National Forests (Los Padres, Angeles, San Bernardino and Cleveland). Running parallel, perpendicular and diagonal to each other these tangled highlands stand ready to absorb, delight and awe flatlanders.

On other days, when the devils send hot, nerve-jangling Santa Ana winds sweeping through mountain passes and pushing the smog to sea, residents also remember that beyond the towering divides lie some 16 million acres of desert lands. Running 240 miles from Death Valley to the Mexican border and 75 to 200 miles wide, the arid county ranges in elevation from —235 feet at the Salton Sea to 7500 feet in the Little San Bernardino Mountains. With less than 10 inches of rainfall a year, these wastes manage to support more than 700 species of flowering plants and nearly 700 species of animals—not to mention lettuce fields and a burgeoning number of humans.

When planning a touring itinerary for your guests, don't forget that year-round the mountains, and in season the deserts, offer special recreational and sightseeing opportunities—and all are within a few hours' drive of downtown Los Angeles. True, mountain streams are sometimes clotted with beer cans, and here and there desert floors have been pocked by trash dumps and permanently marked by motorcycle trails. Still, beyond the city are literally thousands of places where you and your visitors can escape the metropolitan landscape and discover natural forms that are, in a word, prodigious. On weekdays there are hundreds of backroads you can drive almost alone. And there are hideaways aplenty where you can drink deeply of the scent of pine or creosote and listen quietly for the rustle of a blue jay or the whisper of a breeze in mesquite.

Unfortunately, a brief introductory guide like this can merely skim the surface of the mountains and deserts. (More detailed guides are available at any good bookstore.) Instead, this chapter only attempts to make a few suggestions of where and how to sample a bit of real adventure and explore these regions where the romance of the Old West was and, to a remarkable degree, still is.

MOUNTAIN COUNTRY

"I'm going over the hill," a resident of the San Fernando Valley says when he has to go to the Los Angeles basin. By "hill" he means the Santa Monica Mountains, a 50-mile-long range that rises out of the sea at Point Mugu and abruptly ends at the Golden State Freeway. A resource with dozens of factions fighting over their future, the Santa Monicas just might become our first urban national park—a park that could well be the most heavily used in the country. As yet, there is not a great deal to invite the outsider. A drive along dusty Mulholland Drive from Encino to Topanga Canyon Boulevard can illustrate, ad nauseum, what the word chaparral means. Motoring along busy Malibu Canyon Road from the coast to the Ventura Freeway takes you into a breathtaking gorge and through a tunnel above which agile artists have left their marks—first a 20-foot nymphlike nude (quickly whitewashed over), and more recently a smaller Mickey Mouse.

Much more alluring, the San Gabriels are traversed by a network of roads including the Angeles Crest Highway—a high-gear route you can climb on in La Canada and hop off 63 miles later at the Cajon Pass. And in between you will have seen a lot of tall country, like 9399-foot Mt. Baden-Powell which has some 1000-year-old limber pines, and 10,064-foot Mt. San Antonio (Old Baldy) whose ski lift runs all year, with or without snow below.

Or if you take the turnoff at Red Box Gap and go the five extra miles southeast to Mt. Wilson, you might see everything from the Pomona Valley to the San Fernando Valley—if you come at night or on a reasonably clear day. An adage as old as the first member of the L.A. Booster Club says that from this point you can see all the way to Catalina Island, some 64 miles distant. That was true in 1864 when "Don Benito" Wilson supposedly hiked to the 5710-foot peak from Pasadena below, and in 1909 when the 60-inch telescope was installed here under the direction of George Ellery Hale. And it's true today. At least the men and women who work the snack pavilion at Mt. Wilson Skyline Park say you can see the *bottom* of Catalina "maybe once or twice a year." As for the *top* of the island, they report there are many days when it pokes its head above the smog.

Mt. Wilson Skyline Park is an attractive layout (crowded on weekends) with picnic spots, viewpoints and a children's petting zoo and playground—all operated by Metromedia, the conglomerate that includes KTTV, Channel 11. But KTTV is not alone on the mountain. Every single show seen on TV screens in the

119

Los Angeles area comes by way of Mt. Wilson, and the forest of pine, fir and cedar atop the mountain is interrupted by a man-made metallic forest of spindly antennas. The park charges $2 per car, a fee that apparently must be paid to get to the complex of observatories operated by the Carnegie Institute of Washington. Here is the 60-inch telescope, a 100-inch reflector (second largest in the world), two solar telescopes and a small museum.

East of Cajon Pass loom the still taller and more heavily populated and visited San Bernardino Mountains. Reached mainly by the Rim of the World Highway out of "San Berdoo," these mountains are famous for winter sports and summer resorts like Crestline, Lake Arrowhead and Big Bear. For guests with an historical bent there is the Holcomb Valley area behind Big Bear where one of the gold boom camps of the 1860's sprang up—then totally vanished. People still come here with their doodlebugs and sluice boxes to winnow placer gold from the sand, but the results are not enough to cause a 9-to-5 journeyman butcher or baker to leave home and seek a mountain fortune.

A fine all-weather highway connects Big Bear with the Barton Flats area in the San Bernardinos. This is the jumpoff to the tallest peak in Southern California, Mt. San Gorgonio (Old Grayback). You can park at Poop-Out Hill and hike to the 11,502-foot granite summit, where you really will be pooped out. But don't even think of it if you turn purple climbing a flight of stairs at sea level.

From the city of Banning an Alpine-type mountain highway climbs into the pine and lake country of the San Jacinto Mountains, bringing you to the fair mountain settlement of Idyllwild. Just over the mountains is Palm Springs. You can't walk to it—at least not in a straight line. So take instead the Pines to Palms Highway that winds 36 miles from Mountain Center at

4444 feet down to Palm Desert at 223 feet. It's wild, but safe.

For a more dramatic view of the San Jacintos, and an exciting if possibly queasy experience, don't miss a trip on the Palm Springs Aerial Tramway. From Valley Station to Mountain Station it's a silky-smooth, 15-minute ride that takes you *up* 5873 feet in elevation and *down* about 40 degrees in temperature. On a spring day, when wildflowers carpet Chino Canyon and the weather is in the shirtsleeve seventies, you may arrive at the 8516-foot crest to find snow on the ground and temperatures in the 30's. In winter, when you leave Valley Station in a light sweat, temperature in the low 50's, you can step onto the mountain and find your nose numb in the 10-degree air. So dress accordingly. And should you find the ride unsettling, be reassured —food and *drinks* await you.

The Santa Ana Mountains of Orange County offer little in the way of lofty scenic attractions. The old mining camp of Silverado has a long history, and some dreamers still hope that the silver boom will come back. To the south, at the end of Modjeska Canyon Road, you can hike nature trails and do your birdwatching thing at the Tucker Wildlife Sanctuary.

The Palomar Mountains have elevation, stands of cedar, Coulter pine and black oak, a state park with campgrounds and picnic areas, Forest Service recreational facilities, and the Palomar Observatory—a huge silent silver dome housing the world's largest telescope. Brought up the specially constructed Highway to the Stars in 1948, the 200-inch reflector catches the rays of stars one billion light years away. There's a fine small museum here. And viewing the telescope from the visitors' gallery can bring on humbling thoughts.

Down San Diego way the mountain gem is Julian, another gold boom camp now wonderfully faded and alive, nostalgic and refreshing. South of Julian, Cuyamaca Rancho State Park is a delightful wooded parkland hiding the old Stonewall Jackson Mine, one of the top gold producers in San Diego County.

DESERT LANDS

The deserts aren't for everyone. But those who find beauty in their austerity, freedom in their spaces and healing in their silence love these dry places with what borders on fanaticism.

If your guests are potential "desert rats," if they come in winter or early spring, and if they have enough time for an overnight trip to the deserts, then take them first to Joshua Tree National Monument. This half-million-acre preserve just east of the San Bernardino Mountains is uniquely situated on the invisible line that divides the low Colorado Desert to the south and the high Mojave Desert to the north. On the low side you find ocotillo, creosote and palo verde and smoke trees. On the high side you see Mojave yucca and Joshua trees—the strange plants of the lily family for which the monument was named. And in between there are the transitional juniper and cholla, whose "jumping" sections are full of needles that have been painfully known to penetrate leather shoes.

First-time visitors should choose the Twentynine Palms entry where the monument's headquarters and visitor center are located. Here you can obtain literature on the history and ecology of the area, directions on how to find the Lost Horse Mine or how to get to 5185-foot Salton View from where you can see the Salton Sea. Available, too, are information on camping and maps for self-guided nature trails and drives.

The best time to come is in April when the Joshua trees begin to blossom, and you can stay overnight at Twentynine Palms or Joshua Tree on the north, or at Palm Springs or Indio to the south. (Indio is known for its date farms and the National Date Festival held each February. While you sip a date milk shake,

122

you might want to contemplate how these trees are pollinated by hand.).

If Joshua Tree National Monument is a desert-in-the-rough open to all, Palm Springs is the ultimate in civilized desert oases for those of more than comfortable means. Thanks to the vagaries of fortune, even the native Agua Caliente Indians, who own alternate square-mile plots of land, do very well. Ninety-nine-year leases to white men, for establishments like The Spa hotel, produce enough revenues to make a few of them among the wealthiest Indians in the nation.

Once called an extension of Hollywood, and now just as much an arm of Beverly Hills, Palm Springs has spectacular golf courses (almost all private), shops (the best, thank you), swimming pools (refreshing by day or night) and a backdrop of mountains so perfect as to be a Hollywood set designer's dream. It also has scorching summer days, freezing winter nights and annoying winds almost anytime. Outside the city you can explore Indian canyons where stands of native Washingtonia palms thrive, take the Tram up the side of Mt. San Jacinto, or ride horses along sandy washes where quail march about their daily business.

To the south of Palm Springs is Anza-Borrego Desert State Park, another half-million-acre preserve with a long and colorful history and a varied, low-desert terrain. Come in April when the spiny ocotillo and the cholla show off their blossoms. You can camp in virtually any wash—and never worry about getting lost —or stay at Borrego Springs, a pleasant town completely surrounded by the park.

Northeast of Los Angeles, behind the shield of the San Gabriels and the San Bernardinos, lies the larger, wedge-shaped Mojave Desert. You can reach it through Cajon Pass, passing on to Apple Valley (where Roy Rogers and Dale Evans maintain a

123

museum of "memorabilia" including the real, stuffed Trigger), or on to Calico Ghost Town near Yermo (an old silver-mine town redone for the tourist trade with a mine ride, tots' train and sno-cones), or on to Las Vegas.

From Cajon Pass you can cut northwestward along a chain of all-weather roads that skirt the southern edge of the Mojave and follow close aside the famous San Andreas Fault Line. You may tell guests with an interest in geology that the western side of the earthquake-producing fault is moving northward at the rate of 20 feet per century, a remarkable and frightening shift whose effects are plainly visible looking southeast from the city of Valyermo. Stop, too, at the nearby Devil's Punchbowl to picnic among tilted slices of sandstone.

Following State Highway 14 from the San Fernando Valley plops you down into Antelope Valley, the westernmost end of the Mojave. You won't see any antelope in this valley. The herds of yesteryear are gone forever. But if you come in late March or April you will see fields of California poppies, lupine and other wildflowers carpeting the Lancaster and Hi-Vista areas. State Highway 138 from Lancaster to Gorman nearly always presents a colorful display, and the Lancaster Chamber of Commerce operates a free Wildflower Information Center at the fairgrounds where you can find out just where the flowers are blooming that year.

East of Lancaster is Saddleback Buttes State Park, an undeveloped preserve protecting the plants that used to be more common in this part of the valley. And not far from it is the Antelope Valley Indian Museum, a privately owned and operated collection of Indian artifacts set against the rocks of Piute Butte (where, the owner ruefully allows, the Piute Indians never lived).

Guests with incipient gold fever will want to go to Burton's Tropico Gold Mine and Mill, the only large one of its kind open

124

to the public in California. Found 15 miles north of Lancaster and 5 miles west of Rosamond, the mine was an important gold producer from 1896 to 1942. And the custom mill, the largest in Southern California, processed ore from as many as 400 other mines in 1939—its peak year of operation.

Shut down in 1956, Tropico sat silent and useless until Glen and Dorene Burton Settle, the present owners, opened it up for public tours. Downslope they also created a Goldcamp made up of historic buildings—an assay office, miner's cabin, post office, barber shop, livery stable and the like—brought from other locations and restored and arranged with graceful authenticity. Without kiddie rides and such, Tropico isn't exactly the gold mine Knott's Berry Farm is. But the admission fees do buy you a unique and informed look into the past. From October to May there are guided tours of the mine and mill, Thursday through Monday; and the Goldcamp and Museum are open Saturday and Sunday. In summer only the mine, with its 900-foot shaft, is open Thursday through Monday. If your guests come the first weekend in March, bring them here for the annual World Championship Gold Panning Contest. What better souvenir to take home than a little golden stuff from the Golden State.

If you return to Los Angeles by way of the Antelope Valley Freeway, you might want to stop off at Vasquez Rocks—the most famous rock formation in Southern California. Even if your guests haven't heard of them before, you can be reasonably sure they have *seen* them—in countless movies and installments of *Gunsmoke*. Like the Devil's Punchbowl, these layers of sedimentary rock have been compressed and lifted almost on end, making an exciting playground for older, sure-footed children and, so the story goes, was once the hideout for the infamous *bandito* Vasquez. It is operated as a state and county park.

127

$1.95 EACH—WESTERN TRAVEL & LEISURE BOOKS FROM THE WARD RITCHIE PRESS
Trips for the Day, Week-end or Longer
ALL BOOKS COMPLETE, MOST WITH PHOTOGRAPHS AND MAPS

QUANTITY		TOTAL
☐	**BACKYARD TREASURE HUNTING**	$ _____
☐	**BAJA CALIFORNIA:** Vanished Missions, Lost Treasures, Strange Stories-True and Tall	$ _____
☐	**BICYCLE TOURING IN LOS ANGELES**	$ _____
☐	**EAT,** A Toothsome Tour of L.A.'s Specialty Restaurants	$ _____
☐	**EXPLORING BIG SUR, CARMEL AND MONTEREY**	$ _____
☐	**EXPLORING CALIFORNIA BYWAYS, #1** From Kings Canyon to the Mexican Border	$ _____
☐	**EXPLORING CALIFORNIA BYWAYS, #2** In and Around Los Angeles	$ _____
☐	**EXPLORING CALIFORNIA BYWAYS, #3** Desert Country	$ _____
☐	**EXPLORING CALIFORNIA BYWAYS, #4** Mountain Country	$ _____
☐	**EXPLORING CALIFORNIA BYWAYS, #5** Historic Sites of California	$ _____
☐	**EXPLORING CALIFORNIA BYWAYS, #6** Owens Valley	$ _____
☐	**EXPLORING CALIFORNIA BYWAYS, #7** An Historical Sketchbook	$ _____
☐	**EXPLORING CALIFORNIA FOLKLORE**	$ _____
☐	**EXPLORING SMALL TOWNS, No. 1—**Southern California	$ _____
☐	**EXPLORING SMALL TOWNS, No. 2—**Northern California	$ _____
☐	**EXPLORING THE UNSPOILED WEST, Vol. 1**	$ _____
☐	**EXPLORING THE UNSPOILED WEST, Vol. 2**	$ _____
☐	**FEET FIRST:** Walks through ten Los Angeles areas	$ _____
☐	**GREAT BIKE TOURS IN NORTHERN CALIFORNIA**	$ _____
☐	**GUIDEBOOK TO LOST WESTERN TREASURE**	$ _____
☐	**GUIDEBOOK TO THE DELTA COUNTRY OF CENTRAL CALIFORNIA**	$ _____
☐	**GUIDEBOOK TO THE COLORADO DESERT OF CALIFORNIA**	$ _____
☐	**GUIDEBOOK TO THE FEATHER RIVER COUNTRY**	$ _____
☐	**GUIDEBOOK TO THE LAKE TAHOE COUNTRY, Vol. I.** Echo Summit, Squaw Valley and the California Shore	$ _____
☐	**GUIDEBOOK TO THE LAKE TAHOE COUNTRY, Vol. II.** Alpine County, Donner-Truckee, and the Nevada Shore	$ _____
☐	**GUIDEBOOK TO LAS VEGAS**	$ _____

[SEE MORE BOOKS AND ORDER FORM ON OTHER SIDE]

☐	**GUIDEBOOK TO THE MOJAVE DESERT OF CALIFORNIA,** **Vol. 1**—The Western Mojave	$ _____
☐	**GUIDEBOOK TO THE MOJAVE DESERT OF CALIFORNIA,** **Vol. 2**—The Eastern, Includes Death Valley & Joshua Tree National Monuments	$ _____
☐	**GUIDEBOOK TO THE MOUNTAINS OF SAN DIEGO AND** **ORANGE COUNTIES**	$ _____
☐	**GUIDEBOOK TO THE NORTHERN CALIFORNIA COAST,** **VOL. I.** Highway 1	$ _____
☐	**GUIDEBOOK TO THE NORTHERN CALIFORNIA COAST,** **VOL. II.** Humboldt and Del Norte Counties	$ _____
☐	**GUIDEBOOK TO PUGET SOUND**	$ _____
☐	**GUIDEBOOK TO RURAL CALIFORNIA**	$ _____
☐	**GUIDEBOOK TO THE SAN BERNARDINO MOUNTAINS OF** **CALIFORNIA,** Including Lake Arrowhead and Big Bear	$ _____
☐	**GUIDEBOOK TO THE SAN GABRIEL MOUNTAINS OF CALIFORNIA**	$ _____
☐	**GUIDEBOOK TO THE SAN JACINTO MOUNTAINS OF CALIFORNIA**	$ _____
☐	**GUIDEBOOK TO SOUTHERN CALIFORNIA FOSSIL HUNTING**	$ _____
☐	**GUIDEBOOK TO THE SOUTHERN CALIFORNIA SALTWATER** **FISHING**	$ _____
☐	**GUIDEBOOK TO THE SOUTHERN SIERRA NEVADA,** Including Sequoia National Forest	$ _____
☐	**GUIDEBOOK TO VANCOUVER ISLAND**	$ _____
☐	**NATURE AND THE CAMPER.** A Guide to Safety and Enjoyment for Campers and Hikers in the West.	$ _____
☐	**TREES OF THE WEST:** Identified at a Glance.	$ _____
☐	**WHERE TO TAKE YOUR CHILDREN IN NEVADA**	$ _____
☐	**WHERE TO TAKE YOUR CHILDREN IN NORTHERN CALIFORNIA**	$ _____
☐	**WHERE TO TAKE YOUR CHILDREN IN SOUTHERN CALIFORNIA**	$ _____
☐	**WHERE TO TAKE YOUR GUESTS IN SOUTHERN CALIFORNIA**	$ _____
☐	**YOUR LEISURE TIME . . . HOW TO ENJOY IT**	$ _____

WARD RITCHIE PRESS
3044 Riverside Drive, Los Angeles, Calif. 90039

Please send me the Western Travel and Leisure Books I have checked.
I am enclosing $_____, (check or money order). Please include 25¢
per copy to cover mailing costs. California residents add state sales tax.

Name _____

Address _____

City _____ State _____ Zip Code _____